BEYOND
SARAH
AND SAM

By the same authors

Beyond Jennifer & Jason: An Enlightened Guide to Naming Your Baby

Beyond Charles & Diana: An Anglophile's Guide to Baby Naming

Beyond Shannon & Sean: An Enlightened Guide to Irish Baby Naming

BEYOND SARAH AND SAM

AN ENLIGHTENED GUIDE TO JEWISH BABY NAMING

• • • • • • • • • • • • •

LINDA ROSENKRANTZ
& PAMELA REDMOND SATRAN

St. Martin's Press
New York

Library of Congress Cataloging-in-Publication Data

Rosenkrantz, Linda.
  Beyond Sarah & Sam : an enlightened guide to Jewish baby naming
Linda Rosenkrantz and Pamela Redmond Satran.
    p. cm.
    ISBN 0-312-06903-0—ISBN 0-312-06904-9 (pbk.)
    1. Names, Personal—Jewish. 1. Satran, Pamela Redmond.
II. Title. III. Title: Beyond Sarah and Sam.
CS3010.R58 1992
929.4'089924—dc20   91-39250
                                                              CIP

First edition: March 1992

10 9 8 7 6 5 4 3 2 1

CONTENTS

ACKNOWLEDGMENTS   VII

INTRODUCTION   IX

TRADITION AND SUPERSTITION   1

A SHORT HISTORY OF JEWISH NAMES   **3**

MYTHS AND BUBBA MIESSES   **8**

I NEED A GREAT NAME STARTING WITH *H*   **10**

ONLY IN AMERICA   25

AMERICAN JEWISH STYLE   **27**

THE KOSHER CURVE   **29**

SO FAR IN THEY'RE OUT   **33**

SO MANY SARAHS **36**

FASHIONABLE CLASSICS **38**

BUBBA AND ZAYDE NAMES **40**

LAUDERDALE LIMBO **43**

SO FAR OUT THEY'LL ALWAYS BE OUT **46**

THEIR CROWD **48**

HEBRAICA 57

THE GOOD BOOK OF NAMES **59**

HAIFA-NATED NAMES **68**

DESERT BLOOMS **72**

SHABBAT SHALOM, SHABBAT **75**

YIDDISH LIT I **78**

A MIXED MARRIAGE OF NAMES 83

STAR (OF DAVID) SEARCH 91

REEL NAME OR REAL? **93**

MOVIE MOGUL NAMES **96**

JEWISH JOCKS **98**

INDEX OF GIRLS' NAMES 107

INDEX OF BOYS' NAMES 111

ABOUT THE AUTHORS 115

Acknowledgments

Our thanks go first to our editor at St. Martin's, Hope Dellon, for her unfailing support and perceptive input, and to Abigail Kamen for many valuable suggestions, as well as to our equally supportive agent, Molly Friedrich. Thanks also to David Szonyi, for his informed reading of the text. Our appreciation too, for sharing their knowledge of the subject, to Marian and Marty Golan, Marjorie Adoff Cohen, and those generous Lauderdale Lakers—Fran Rosenkrantz, Harry and Liliane Seligman, Claire Ellner, and Selta Stein. As always, we are grateful to our husbands, Christopher Finch and Richard Satran, for continuing to understand the obsession, and to our wonderful children, Chloe Finch, Rory Satran, and Joe Satran.

We would also like to acknowledge our appreciation of and reliance on the scholarly research of Benzion C. Kaganoff, Alfred J. Kolatch, and Smadar Shir Sidi.

INTRODUCTION

You want to name your baby after your grandfather
Moishe, but it seems as if all the "good" M names—those
that appeal to both the Jewish person and the modern parent in you, names like Max and Molly and Melissa and
even Michael—have become overused. Or you want to give
your child a biblical name, but every time you open the
Old Testament you seem to be faced with a choice between
the usual Sarahs and Adams and the beyond-the-pale Jeze-
bels and Jobabs.

Maybe you've become deeply religious in recent years and
want a thoroughly Hebrew or Israeli name, but you can't find
a wide selection. Or maybe you're married to a non-Jew and
want a name that offers the same kind of compromise as the
Star of David atop your Christmas tree.

Whatever your considerations in choosing a name for your
baby, you've got a problem. The standard retinue of naming
dictionaries offers plenty of names with Hebrew origins but
gives no guidance as to which of these are appropriate for a

INTRODUCTION

Jewish-American baby. And books of "Jewish" names often narrow your field too much, listing appropriate Hebrew and Israeli names but ignoring hundreds of others—even basics like Harry and Charles and Susan—that have traditionally been used and accepted by Jews.

We know firsthand the frustration of wanting a certain kind of name but having to sift through mounds of irrelevant information to find it. That frustration is part of what inspired our first baby-naming book, *Beyond Jennifer & Jason: An Enlightened Guide to Naming Your Baby.* In *Beyond Jennifer & Jason,* we group names not alphabetically but according to parents' real-life requirements and concerns: fashionable names and ambisexual names and biblical names and, yes, Hebrew names.

But while *Beyond Jennifer & Jason* has proven the perfect primer for parents interested in narrowing down the whole wide world of names, those parents whose name focus is tighter—who are interested only in Jewish names, for instance—want more. Rather than a handful of Jewish names within a universal name book, they want a universe of Jewish names from which to choose.

That's where this book comes in. *Beyond Sarah & Sam*— beyond, in other words, the obvious choices—is the first Jewish baby-naming book to offer the innovative structure that has made its parent, *Beyond Jennifer & Jason,* so popular. The array of chapters and lists you'll find here—from ultra-trendy Jewish names to those just coming into style, from Jewish naming traditions to the names that honor them, from biblical names to Israeli names to names that successfully marry Jewish and Christian cultures—can help you to not only understand the full range of Jewish names but to find the perfect one for your child. This material is organized into five major sections:

Tradition and Superstition: How did Marvin, originally Welsh, come to be considered a Jewish name? Why are some New Testament names, Mark or Matthew, say, well used among Jews, while others, such as Mary, usually avoided? Who says you have to name your baby after a dead relative, anyway? And if you have to, are there any great names starting with H? In this section you'll find insights into Jewish naming traditions and superstitions through the ages, plus a comprehensive list of names that offer the perfect compromise between style and tradition.

Only in America: A look at Jewish naming style in America, from the days our bubbas and zaydes stepped off the boat to the present. Here, you'll find guidance on which names are trendy (some would say *too* trendy) among young Jewish parents, which are untouchable, and which are prime for a fashion comeback.

Hebraica: In this section we turn away from the secular world to the Bible, to Israel, and to classic Yiddish literature. Here, a complete list of good names from the Good Book, plus some bad ones; an overview of Israeli names; and a whole shtetl of names from Isaac Bashevis Singer.

A Mixed Marriage of Names: He's Jewish, she's not, or vice versa. This section offers a wide range of names to satisfy both your families and both your tastes—and possibly save your marriage.

Star (of David) Search: A compendium of Jewish athletes and stars, and the names they made famous.

Many of the names in this book are as familiar as family, and many others—particularly those in the Hebraica section—you may be seeing for the first time. Likewise, some of the names here may strike you as appealingly fresh, others may seem simply weird. Where you draw the line, and on which side of it you choose to stand, is up to you. What you'll get from this book is the full complement of Jewish names, and in the end, the pleasure of knowing you've made a thoughtful and enlightened choice, whether you decide to move beyond Sarah and Sam or not.

TRADITION
AND
SUPERSTITION

A SHORT HISTORY OF JEWISH NAMES

But wait. What is a Jewish name anyway? Is it the Biblical Hebrew Avraham or the Yiddish Avrum or the Anglicized Abraham? Is it Joseph, the Old Testament patriarch—but also the New Testament husband of the Virgin Mary? Is it a name like Isidore (a common ancient Greek name and that of a seventh-century saint) adopted from another culture and now the almost exclusive property of the Jews? Is it the much maligned Marvin (originally Welsh), or the schleppified Seymour or Stanley, both of which had their beginnings as aristocratic British surnames?

Obviously, there is no simple answer to the question, no all-encompassing definition. The story of Jewish naming practices is in fact the history of Jewish attitudes through the ages, of assimilation and alienation, of conformity and creativity.

For Jews, given names have always been potent statements, invested with layers of rich symbolic tradition. Beginning in the early biblical period, Hebrew names were bestowed with a keen awareness of their meaning. Jewish children, like children in many other cultures, were given names that reflected some event, public or familial, that happened around the time of their birth, or some characteristic peculiar to the baby, or else they were given names that were expressions of some religious or moral truth or aspiration.

Looking at the Bible itself, we see first of all that names were strictly one to a customer. There was one Adam, one Eve, one Cain and one Abel in the Old Testament, a fact that held true for over a thousand years, during which time there was no reappearance of those names or of any of the others that would later be so common—no Davids, Benjamins, Rachels, or Rebeccas. As a matter of fact, biblical names were not readily accepted for general use until the Reformation period. Before the Reformation, names were exclusive properties, belonging and relating solely to the person to whom they were first applied, never passed on from generation to generation.

The Bible also illustrates the weight and iconic significance with which names were infused. In the opening pages, Adam's first charge is the naming of every beast of the fields and bird of the heavens. And the scriptural names for humans were even more carefully chosen to reflect the relationship of the bearer to God (Joshua: the Lord is my Salvation), a desirable quality (Hannah: gracious, merciful), or a symbol of a desirable quality (Rachel: a ewe, representing gentleness). When a biblical personage was to make a major change of identity or take a new path in the course of leadership, he or she was almost always given a new name. Thus, for example, Sarai became Sarah and Abram became Abraham when they entered into their covenant with God. The new name signified the fact of becoming, in essence, a new person.

Wanted: A Name, Dead or Alive

It wasn't until after the destruction of the First Temple and the taking of the Jews into Babylonian captivity that Palestinian Jews began to adopt the Egyptian custom of naming children after deceased relatives. In the Talmudic period (70 B.C.E. to 500 C.E.) the circle of honorees widened to include living parents and grandparents and other relatives and friends. It was also around this time that special names started to be conferred on children born on holidays or other special days, for example, Esther for girls born on Purim. (For others see Shabbat Shalom, Shabbat, page 75.)

But here a dichotomy grew up between the Ashkenazic Jews—those from Central and Eastern Europe—and the Sephardim—Jews from Spain and Portugal, the Balkan countries, North Africa, and the Middle East. It was the former who around the fourth or fifth century B.C.E adopted the practice of naming their children after a deceased relative, thus preserving the ancestor's memory, perpetuating a community of all who had gone before, and—no small matter—not encroaching on the soul that was intrinsically bound up with a living person's name. (For a discussion of the superstitious elements involved, see Myths and Bubba Miesses, page 8.) Contrary to popular belief, there are no rules in Jewish law mandating this, and no mention of it in the Bible. This custom continues to the present day, however, and is practiced in any of the following ways:

1. By using the exact Hebrew or Yiddish name of the deceased.
2. By picking a modern name with the same initial sound as

the Hebrew name (for some suggestions, see I Need a Great Name Starting with *H* on page 10.)
3. By finding a name with an equivalent meaning in English or modern Hebrew.

A Word to the Wise

One should examine names carefully in order to give his son a name that is worthy so that the son may become a righteous person.

The Midrash

Sephardic Jews, on the other hand, had no qualms about naming their children in honor of a living grandparent or even parent—in fact they believed that this would lengthen the life of the older relative. Before long, a rather rigid protocol evolved: the oldest grandson was named for his paternal grandfather, the oldest granddaughter for her paternal grandmother, whether the grandparents were living or dead. Subsequent offspring were named for their maternal grandparents, followed by aunts and uncles.

THE SACRED AND THE SECULAR

Almost from the beginning, there has been a tendency for Jews to adopt and adapt the names of their host countries.

At first Gentile names were employed only for interaction with non-Jews, but gradually they came to be used more and more extensively, until the Hebrew names became almost extinct. In fear of losing them altogether—especially since it was believed that Hebrew was the lingua franca of Heaven— the rabbinate decreed that every Jewish boy be given two names: one civil, for use in his everyday business life, the other Jewish (Hebrew or Yiddish) to be used in religious ceremonies, such as being called up to the Torah for his Bar Mitzvah and in marriage contracts. Since women were not called to the Torah, there was no necessity for them to have two names although in practice they did so even more than men. The custom of double-naming—again, a custom, not a religious stricture—still persists today, albeit no longer in its sexist form.

Myths and Bubba Miesses

The bestowing and changing of names plays a significant role in the demon-filled drama of Jewish folklore. And many of the superstitions have to do with trying to trick the Angel of Death. After all, there was a heartwrenchingly high infant-mortality rate in ancient times, and parents would go to any lengths to protect their newborns from the demons who seemed intent on snatching their babies away. In order to fool the Angel of Death, a curiously literal entity who chose victims strictly by name and address, or of Lilith, a vampirelike demon who roamed the earth searching for Jewish babies, sickly infants might be given an affirmative name like Chayim (life) or Selig (blessed) or one associated with old age (Alte, Zayda) as a camouflage, in the hopes that Death would then pass them by. And since Jewish children were known by their parents' names as well (Rebecca, daughter of Isaac), further protection was provided by also changing the names of the parents—not by actually renaming them but by symbolically "selling" the child to another family, thereby *totally* confusing the Angel of Death. By the same token, the Ashkenazim would be careful not to take the name of a living relative, so the child wouldn't be mistakenly abducted in place of its grandparent, while Sephardim, as mentioned, do name their children after the living.

There was another, more spiritual, reason for not using the name of a living person. The ancients believed that a person's name represented the essence of his or her being, so that to transfer the name of one living entity to another would, in fact, be robbing the first one of his or her identity; without a name, he or she would no longer exist.

But within the name resided not only the essence of the person but also his destiny, which led to another whole series of superstitions. It was considered foolhardy to name a child after someone who had died a violent death or who had died young or childless, or for parents to use the name of a child of their own who had died.

In his book, A Dictionary of Jewish Names and Their History, Rabbi Benzion C. Kaganoff describes a curious folk custom adopted by early German Jews from a Gentile myth revolving around a demon witch called Holle who carried off infants. In order for the demon to be repelled, a naming ceremony called Holle Kreisch (meaning to encircle Holle) was held on the fourth Sabbath after the child's birth. Children would be invited to the new baby's home, where they would form a circle around its cradle. The baby was then lifted into the air three times as the guests shouted, "Hollekreisch! What shall the child's name be?" and answered with the name of the child. The child was thus protected against the evil spirit.

I NEED A GREAT NAME STARTING WITH *H*

When our book *Beyond Jennifer & Jason* came out, Jewish parents in search of naming advice would cut right to the chase: "I need a great name," they'd say, "but it has to start with an *M*." Or a *J* or an *H* or an *E*. The point was that they were restricted to names that began with a single initial, because they were honoring a deceased relative. But even working within that narrow framework, they still wanted a name that was "kosher" in every way: a name that was in keeping with their Jewish heritage but was also identifiably "American"; a name that wasn't too unusual, wasn't too frumpy, but also wasn't overly trendy.

Wow! Quite a list of requirements! But there aren't as few names that fit the bill on all counts as you might guess. Some of the names that follow are traditional Hebrew or Israeli choices that are consistent with American tastes; others, while not strictly "Jewish" names, are also not strictly Christian ones and have been judged acceptable by Jewish parents.

We've avoided overly ethnic Hebrew, Israeli, and Yiddish names as well as overly ethnic names of other persuasions: no Seans, Kellys, Francescas, Duncans, Kirstens, Winstons, or

Parkers. We haven't included too-trendy names favored by Jewish parents, such as Sam, Max, Jessica, and Rachel, nor names that are too trendy in general—no Heathers, Tiffanys, Jasons, or Kyles. And though we have left in such currently popular classics as David and Daniel and Elizabeth and Laura, poor Michael and Sarah, which theoretically belong in the same timeless class, have been eliminated due to rampant overuse.

Still, we haven't gone overboard in eliminating any one type of name. We figure that among the thousands of modern Jewish parents out there, some will be comfortable with a name as ethnic as Michal or as goyish as Martha, as stylish as Molly, as traditional as Miriam, or as charmingly offbeat as Matilda.

Here's proof that you don't have to choose between honoring your Tante Tsika and giving your child the perfect name:

G I R L S

A

ABIGAIL
ABRA
ADINA
ADRIENNE
ALEXA
ALICE
ALIZA
ALLEGRA
AMELIA
ANDREA
ANNA
ANNABEL
ANNE
ARABELLA
ARIELLA
AUGUSTA
AVIVA

B
=

BEATRICE	BESS
BEATRIX	

C
=

CAMILLA	CHLOE
CARMEL(A)	CLAIRE
CAROLINE	CLARISSA
CELIA	CLAUDIA
CHARLOTTE	CLEA

D
=

DAHLIA	DELILAH
DAISY	DEVORAH
DALE	DIANA
DANA	DIANTHA
DARIA	DINAH
DAVIDA	DORA
DEBORAH	DORIAN
DELIA	DOROTHEA

E

=

EDEN	ELIZABETH
EDITH	ELLA
ELANA	ELOISE
ELEANOR	EMANUELA
ELIANA	EMILY
ELIORA	EMMA
ELIZA	EVE

F

=

FAY	FRANCES
FLORA	

G

=

GABRIELLA	GEORGINA
GENEVA	GILLIAN
GEORGIA	

H

=

HANNAH	HENRIETTA
HARRIET	HILARY
HELEN	HOPE
HELENA	

I

=

ILANA	ISABELLA
IMOGENE	ISADORA
ISABEL	IVY

J

=

JACOBA	JOANNA
JADE	JOCELYN
JAEL	JOSEPHA
JANE	JOSEPHINE
JASMINE	JUDITH
JEMIMA	JULIA
JENNA	JULIANA
JESSA	JULIET

K

=

KAILA	KELILA
KATE	KETURA(H)
KAYLA	KEZIA(H)

L

LACEY
LAILA
LARISSA
LAURA
LAUREL
LAYLA
LEAH
LEIGH
LEILA
LEONORA

LEORA
LIANA
LIBBY
LILA
LILY
LOUISA
LOUISE
LUCY
LYDIA

M

MADELINE
MAISIE
MARA(H)
MARGOT
MARIAH
MARIAN
MARISSA
MARTHA
MATILDA
MAUD
MEREDITH

MIA
MICHAELA
MICHAL
MILLICENT
MINNIE
MIRABEL
MIRANDA
MIRIAM
MOLLY
MORIAH

N
=

NADYA/NADIA	NESSA
NAOMI	NICOLA
NATASHA	NINA
NELL	NOEMI

O
=

ODELIA	OLIVIA
ODESSA	

P
=

PAULINE	PHOEBE
PEARL	POLLY
PERRY	

Q (Does anyone ever need a *Q*?)

QUINTANA	QUINTINA

R

=

RAE	RINA
RAISA	ROSA
RAMONA	ROSE
RAPHAELA	ROWENA
RAYNA	ROXANNE
REBECCA	RUBY
RENATA	RUTH
RHEA	

S

=

SABRA	SHOSHANA
SABRINA	SIMONE
SACHA	SONIA
SALLY	SOPHIA
SARAI	SOPHIE
SELENA	STELLA
SERENA	SUSANNAH
SHANA	SYDNEY

T

=

TALIA	TILLIE
TAMAR	TOVA
TAMARA	TYNE
THEA	

V
=

VENETIA   VIOLET
VIOLA

W
=

WILLA   WINONA

Y
=

YAEL

Z
=

ZARA   ZIONA
ZELIA   ZOE
ZIA   ZORA

B O Y S

A
=

AARON   ABNER
ABE   ABRAHAM
ABEL   ABRAM

ADLAI
ADRIAN
ALEC
AMORY
AMOS
ANDREW

ARI
ARNO
ASA
ASHER
AVERY
AZA

B
=

BENNO
BOAZ
BRAM

BRUNO
BYRON

C
=

CALEB
CALVIN
CASPAR
CHAIM

CHARLES
CLAUDE
COLE
CONRAD

D
=

DANIEL
DARIUS
DAVID

DAVIS
DEREK
DOV

E

=

EDWARD
ELI
ELIJAH
ELISHA
EMANUEL
EMMETT

ENOCH
EPHRAIM
ESAU
ETHAN
EZEKIEL
EZRA

F

=

FELIX
FRANK

FRAZIER
FREDERICK

G

=

GABRIEL
GARSON
GEORGE

GIDEON
GORDON
GUS

H

=

HARRIS
HARRISON
HARRY

HENRY
HIRAM
HOMER
HOSEA

I
=

ISAAC	ISHMAEL
ISAIAH	ISRAEL

J
=

JABEZ	JOACHIM
JACK	JONAH
JARED	JORDAN
JASPER	JOSEPH
JEDIDIAH	JOSIAH
JEREMIAH	JULIAN
JETHRO	

K
=

KALMAN	KERMIT

L
=

LABAN	LEVI
LEMUEL	LIONEL
LEO	LOUIS/LEWIS
LEV	LOWELL

M
=

MALACHI
MALCOLM
MARCUS
MATTHEW
MATTHIAS

MICAH
MILO
MORRIS
MOSES

N
=

NATHAN
NATHANIEL
NED

NEHEMIAH
NOAH
NOAM

O
=

OLIVER
OREN

ORSON
OZ

P
=

PAUL
PETER

PHINEAS

R

=

RAPHAEL	REX
REUBEN	RUSSELL

S

=

SAMSON	SIMM
SAUL	SIMON
SETH	SOLOMON
SIMEON	SPENCER

T

=

TOBIAH	TOBIAS

U

=

URI	URIAH

W

=

WILL	WYATT
WILLIAM	

Z

=

ZACHARIAH	ZEDEKIAH
ZALMAN	ZEV
ZEBEDIAH	ZVI

ONLY IN AMERICA

AMERICAN JEWISH STYLE

The first Jewish Americans were twenty-five Sephardim who arrived at the Dutch colony of New Amsterdam in 1654. By the time of the Revolutionary War, there were still only about 2,000 Jews in all the Colonies; it wasn't until around 1830 that full-scale Jewish immigration began in earnest. At least a quarter of a million Jews, most of them German, entered the United States in the next fifty years; then, beginning in 1881, after a wave of pogroms in southern Russia, they came in even greater numbers. By the beginning of World War I, there were 1,400,000 Jews crowded into the square mile that formed New York's Lower East Side, making it the largest Jewish community in the world.

When these Jewish immigrants arrived at Ellis Island, many of the Gutmans among them became Goodmans, and some of the Fuchses became Foxes, but for the most part the Gittels and Gedalyahs remained Gittel and Gedalyah. It was in the next generation, the first born in America, that the nomenclature suddenly changed. Following the tradition of using the same initial letter for the English name as for the

Hebrew name, the greenhorn generation looked around for cognates for Moishe and somehow came up with the most elegant Anglo names they could find: Murray (a Scottish surname), Morton and Milton (English surnames), Myron (a Classical Greek name taken up by the early Christians), and Marvin (derived from Old Welsh). Similarly, Itzak became Irwin (English), Isidore (Greek), or Irving (Scottish), while descendants of Schmuel could be Sheldon, Seymour, or Stanley, all aristocratic British surnames. Successive generations pretty much followed mainstream American naming patterns, with some particular favorites (Shirley, Marilyn), and some understandable exceptions (Christina, Patrick).

"Let's see: if it's a boy, we'll name him Christopher after my great-aunt's second husband, Hayim."

"Yeah, and if it's a girl, we'll name her Megan Fern after my father's father, Moishe, and my mother's second cousin Fayge."

Sharon Strassfeld and Michael Strassfeld, *The Second Jewish Catalogue,* The Jewish Publication Society of America, 1976

In this section we look at American Jewish names today, what's in and what's out, which classics will always be in fashion and which names are so far in they're out, as well as those unfortunates that are so far out they'll always be out, and those whose ultimate fate is yet to be decided, as they dangle in what we think of as Lauderdale Limbo.

THE KOSHER CURVE

If you've wondered why there weren't many Sams or Maxes born in the 1950s or 1960s, the explanation lies in what we call the Kosher Curve theory. According to this way of thinking, as part of their effort toward assimilation, first-generation immigrants typically renounce any clue to their ethnicity by choosing names for their children that are prevelant in mainstream society. It is not until the third generation, or even later, that there is enough psychological distance for people to reembrace their ethnic heritage and incorporate it into their lives.

This is evidenced by the naming history of Jewish families in the United States. The children of early immigrants sought the most Anglo-Saxon–sounding names, lighting in particular upon aristocratic British surnames like Stanley and Sheldon, Morton, Milton, and Melvin.

The following chart (updated from the one in *Beyond Jennifer & Jason*) tracks some representative American Jewish given names and their permutations from the turn of the century to the present.

ABE ● ARTHUR ● ALAN ● ADAM ● AARON
ANNA ● ANN ● ANITA ● ANNIE ● ASHLEY
BEN ● BERNARD ● BARRY ● BENJAMIN ● BRENDAN
CLARA ● CLAIRE ● CAROL ● CARRIE ● CLAIRE
DORA ● DOROTHY ● DIANE ● DEBBY ● DAKOTA
HARRY ● HENRY ● HARRIS ● HARRISON ● HARRY
ISAAC ● IRVING ● IRA ● IAN ● ISAAC
JAKE ● JEROME ● JAY ● JASON ● JAKE
JENNY ● JEAN ● JANICE ● JENNIFER ● JENNA
LILLIE ● LILLIAN ● LINDA ● LORI ● LILY
MAX ● MARVIN ● MITCHELL ● MICHAEL ● MAX
MOLLY ● MARIAN ● MARSHA ● MARCY ● MOLLY
NELLIE ● NORMA ● NANCY ● NICOLE ● NELL
RACHEL ● RHODA ● ROCHELLE ● RICKI ● RACHEL
ROSE ● RUTH ● RENÉE ● RANDI ● ROSIE
SADIE ● SYLVIA ● SUSAN ● STACY ● SAMANTHA
SAM ● SIDNEY ● STEVEN ● SCOTT ● SAM
SARA ● SELMA ● SHEILA ● SHELLY ● SARAH
SOPHIE ● SHIRLEY ● SHARON ● SHERRY ● SOPHIA

Sarah to Sara

A Jewish woman I know started in life as Sarah; at sixteen
she became Shirley; at twenty the Greenwich Village
atmosphere in which she lived changed her to Sonia; now
she is Sara.

Louis Adamic, *What's Your Name?* Harper & Brothers,
1942

At Ellis Island we were questioned and examined by immigration officials and told our English names. Because my Polish birth certificate said "Jew-child Carolina" I was dubbed and registered as "Caroline," a barbed-wire fence that divided me from myself throughout my school years. I hated it and would never answer my father when he tried to be fancy and American in public, addressing me by a name that belonged entirely to P.S. 58, P.S. 57, P.S. 59, to Theodore Roosevelt High School, to James Monroe High School, to Hunter College, not to me. How we got to Kate I don't know. My mother must have sought it out to keep as clear as possible the link to her grandmother Kaila, not realizing how intensely Catholic a name it then was.

Kate Simon, *Bronx Primitive,* The Viking Press, New York, 1982

Because I was eight years younger than Donald I was something of a novelty among his friends—like a puppy or a kitten. . . . Their names were Seymour, Bernie, Harold, Stanley, Harvey, Irwin, and so on. In my mind they are like a chorus of noisemakers. Not faces or voices I recall, but horns, bladders, ratchets, and wheezing party favors that someone blows in your face.

E.L. Doctorow, *World's Fair*
Random House, New York, 1985

So far in they're out

A generation ago, the most fashionable names for Jewish babies were the cute, bouncy—and, many might say, flimsy—names that so gripped America's imagination in the fifties and sixties. Frippery such as Shari, Ricki, and Jamie was in, while time-honored Jewish names like Jonathan and Rachel and Jesse and Sarah were cast aside.

Today's Jewish parents have rediscovered the names of their forebears, both ancient—as evidenced by the resurrection of biblical favorites like Joshua and Rebecca—and not so ancient: witness all the little grandma-and-grandpa Maxes and Jakes and Sophies running around. But while most of us would agree that Sam and Sarah are an improvement over Shari and Stacy, the trouble is that this new generation of old names is now threatened by overexposure.

Of course, many parents like giving their child a name that is popular and therefore easily accepted both by the child and by the child's peers. There's much good sense behind this tack: an easy and familiar name can smooth a child's path from day care to grade school through to adulthood. The important thing is to choose a widely used name deliberately—to choose Max knowing there are likely to be three other Maxes in the sandbox—and not to pick Max thinking it's unusual and exotic, only to want to slit your wrists once you discover its prevalence in the playground.

Here, as a warning to those parents looking for a name that's not trendy, and a guide for parents in search of one that is, a list of the most popular—or, depending on your viewpoint, overused—names among Jewish parents today:

G I R L S

ALEXANDRA	ERICA
ALEXIS	HEATHER
ALISON	JENNIFER
ALYSSA (and	JENNY
variations like	JESSICA
ILISSA, ELICIA, etc.)	JESSIE
AMANDA	JORDAN
AMBER	KAYLA
AMY	KIMBERLY
ARIEL	LAUREN
ASHLEY	LINDSAY
BRITTANY	MELISSA
BROOKE	MICHELLE
CARLY	SAMANTHA
COURTNEY	STEPHANIE
DANIELLE	TIFFANY

B O Y S

ADAM	JEREMY
ALEXANDER	JESSE
BEN	JONATHAN
BENJAMIN	JOSHUA
BRANDON	JUSTIN
DUSTIN	LOREN
ERIC	MAX
JACOB	NICHOLAS
JAKE	SAM
JASON	ZACHARY

So many Sarahs

In one of our own typical Jewish-American families, there are four Sarahs—plus one Sarajane—three Rebeccas, three Naomis, two Rachels, two Hannahs, three Davids, two Daniels, a Jeremy, a Joshua, and several generations of Sams. Are there any substitutes for these overused classics? We think there are.

Here are a few examples which bear some relationship to their overexposed counterparts in sound, feel, or taste, but with a color that's brighter and a crisper texture.

GIRLS

Instead of	Consider
ALYSSA	ALICE
ARIEL	ARELLA

DANIELLE .... DELILAH or GABRIELLE
RACHEL .... RUTH or MIRIAM
REBECCA .... RAPHAELA
SARAH .... MARAH or SARAI or (for the bold)
                   SADIE

B O Y S

Instead of   Consider

AARON .... ABEL
ADAM .... ABNER
BENJAMIN .... BENNO
DANIEL .... DARIUS
DAVID .... JARED
JACOB .... CALEB
JAKE .... ABE
JEREMY .... JEREMIAH or JETHRO
JONATHAN .... JONAS or GIDEON
JOSHUA .... JOSIAH
MATTHEW .... MOSES
MAX .... GUS or MOE
MICHAEL .... MICAH
NOAH .... NOAM
SAM .... SAUL or SIMM
SAMUEL .... LEMUEL
SIMON .... SIMEON

FASHIONABLE CLASSICS

While these names are very far in, they'll never really be out, having survived the vicissitudes of fashion throughout the ages. Many are biblical names; others have been used in many variations for generations of children, Jewish and non-Jewish alike. The fashionable classics most in favor among modern Jewish parents are:

GIRLS

ANNA
ELIZABETH
EMILY
JANE
KATE

LAURA
RACHEL
REBECCA
SARAH

B O Y S

ANDREW
CHARLES
DANIEL
DAVID
HENRY

MATTHEW
MICHAEL
PHIL(L)IP
WILLIAM

BUBBA AND ZAYDE NAMES

Okay, we know that when we were little we never dreamed about naming our children the names of our pinochle-playing zaydes or our gemültlich great-grandmas. And yet somehow we grew up to find our neighbors' nurseries filled with Maxes and Jakes, Jessies and Beckys. What will be the next wave to hit that particular shore? We don't, frankly, think the world is ready for an epidemic of Irvings, but we can imagine the following names from that same generation making a comeback:

GIRLS

BEA	BIRDIE
BELLA	BLANCHE
BELLE	CEIL
BESS	CLARA

CORA	LOTTIE
DORA	MILLIE
ESTHER	MIN
ETTA	MIRIAM
EVA	NATALIE
FANNY	NETTIE
FAY	PEARL
GOLDIE	ROSE
IDA	SADIE
LETTY	SOPHIE
LIBBY	TESS
LILY	TILLIE

B O Y S

ABE	LOU
BARNEY	MACK
ELI	MEYER
GUS	MOE
HARRY	MORRIS
HY	MOSES
ISAAC	NAT
ISIDORE	SAUL
ISRAEL	SI
JACK	SIM
KALMAN	SOL
LEO	WILLIE

Another route might be back to the Yiddish. How about these: (See also Yiddish Lit I, page 78.)

G I R L S

BAILE/BAILA/BAYLA	LIBA
BLUMA	MOLKA
BOSHA	NESYA
CHAIA	RAIZEL
CHANA	RAYNA
DVORA/DEVORA	RIVKA
ELKA	SHAYNA
FEYA/FEYGA	SORALI
FRAYDA	SORKE
GITTEL/GITA	SURA
GOLDA	TRESTEL
HINDA	TZIREL
KAYLA	YENTEL
KREINDEL	ZELDE
LAILA/LEYA	

B O Y S

ANSHEL	MICHEL
AVRUM	MOISHE
CHAIM	NUSAN
DOVID	SANDER
HASKEL	SHLOMO
HERSH	YANKEL
ITZAK/ITZIK	YISROEL
LABE	YONKEL
LAZAR	YUDEL
LEIB	YUSSEL
MAYER	ZALMAN
MENDEL	

LAUDERDALE LIMBO

Visit your grandmother in any retirement condominium complex in southern Florida and you're sure to run into a ubiquitous naming phenomenon. Grandma and her canasta mates all have hip-sounding names like Jessie and Molly and Bess (see Bubba and Zayde Names, page 40), and their grandchildren and great-grandchildren respond to the equally trendy Kayla and Chelsea. But caught in the middle, in Lauderdale Limbo, are the names of the Jewish generation in between, names that are not really beyond the pale (see So Far Out They'll Always Be Out, page 46) but are so strongly associated with middle-aged Boomers that they don't sound young enough to bestow on a baby. But they could come back. These include:

G I R L S

ANITA	KAREN
ARLENE	LENORE
AUDREY	LEONORE
BARBARA	LESLIE
BERNICE	LINDA
BONNIE	LISA
BRENDA	LOIS
CAROL	LORETTA
CHERYL	LORI
CINDY	LORRAINE
DAWN	LYNN
DEBBY	MARCIA
DIANE	MARCY
EILEEN	MARILYN
ELAINE	MARJORIE
ELISE	MARLENE
EVELYN	MAXINE
FRANCINE	MINDY
GAIL	MONA
HEIDI	MURIEL
HELENE	NADINE
JANET	NANCY
JANICE	NANETTE
JILL	NORMA
JOAN	PAULA
JOANNE	PHYLLIS
JODY	RANDI
JOY	RHODA
JOYCE	RHONDA
JUDY	RICKI

RITA
ROBERTA
ROSALIE
ROSLYN
SANDRA
SHARON

SHEILA
SHERRY
SUSAN
SUZANNE
SYLVIA
WENDY

B O Y S

ALAN
BARRY
BRUCE
DONALD
ELIOT
EUGENE
GARY
GENE
GILBERT
HOWARD
IRA
JAY
JEFFREY
JOEL
KENNETH

LAWRENCE
MARK
MARSHALL
MARTIN
MITCHELL
NORMAN
ROGER
RONALD
ROY
SCOTT
STEVEN
STUART/STEWART
VICTOR
WALTER
WARREN

So far out they'll always be out

These are the names—we're sorry—that we just don't see making a comeback. And for some reason, though there were more girls' names in Lauderdale Limbo, this list is more heavily weighted on the boys' side. Many of them, we fear, even though they may have the noblest of Anglo-Saxon heritages, have just become too laden down with schleppy images ever to recover.

GIRLS

BERNICE	GOLDA
BERTHA	GUSSIE
EDNA	HESTER
ETHEL	IRMA
FRIEDA	MILDRED
GERTRUDE	MYRNA

SELMA   SIBYL
SHIRLEY   YETTA

B O Y S

ALVIN   MANNY
ARNOLD   MARVIN
BERNARD   MAURICE
BERTRAM   MELVIN
HARVEY   MENDEL
HERBERT   MILTON
HERMAN   MORTON
HERSHEL   MURRAY
HYMAN   MYRON
IRVING   SEYMOUR
IRWIN   SHELDON
JULIUS   SHERMAN
LESTER   SIDNEY
               STANLEY

THEIR CROWD

In 1967, a book called *Our Crowd,* by Stephen Birmingham, was published and almost immediately became a bestseller. It chronicled the saga of the great German-Jewish-American aristocracy, families like the Lehmans, Lewisohns, and Loebs, Strauses, Schiffs, and Seligmans, Guggenheims and Goldmans and Sachs, Warburgs and Kahns—a collective success story in business, banking, and the arts. Many of their names, too, especially in the second and third generations, had a certain Teutonic-elitist ring. Would your child be a future stock market czar, given a name like:

G I R L S

ADELHEID .... Schiff
ALICE .... Lewisohn

ALVA .... Bernheimer
AUGUSTA .... Rosenwald
BABET .... Steinhardt Seligman
BABETTE .... Seligman, Mayer
BERTHA .... Goldman
CAROLA .... Warburg Rothschild
CECILE .... Seligman
CHARLOTTE .... Warburg
CLARA .... Schiff
DVORA .... Warburg
EDA .... Kuhn Loeb
EDITHE .... Neustadt Stralem
ELENA .... Warburg
EMANIE .... Sachs
EMMA .... Cahn Lewisohn, Seligman
FELICIA .... Warburg Sarnoff
FLORETTE .... Seligman Guggenheim
FLORINE .... Seligman
FRIEDA .... Schiff Warburg
GUTA .... Loeb Seligman
HELENE .... Seligman
HENRIETTE .... Seligman
LEONORE .... Seligman Wasserman
LINA .... Seligman
LOUISE .... Goldman Sachs
NIVA .... Warburg
PAULINE .... Lehman
REGINA .... Seligman
REGINE .... Wedeles Seligman
RENATA .... Warburg Straus
ROSA .... Goldman Sachs
ROSALIE .... Seligman
ROSINA .... Loeb
SOPHIA .... Sachs
SOPHIE .... Seligman
TAMA .... Warburg
THERESE .... Loeb Schiff

Times Have Changed

In the April 1931 issue of the *Zeta Beta Tau Quarterly,* there is an article dividing the then current crop of Jewish first names into three categories: biblical, mercantile, and baronial. Examples of the first category, the journal reports, "though not entirely extinct, have about lapsed into disuse." The mercantile names "are those of children who are bound to succeed in the world of affairs. We find," the article goes on to elaborate, "possessors of these names in operators of the cloak and suit industry, and in the smaller towns they are invariably the proprietors of the leading clothing shoppes. Generally, the bearer of a mercantile name, *viz.* Julius, Max, Emanuel, Gus or Nathan, is a representative constituent of our most conservative and substantial citizenry."

The baronial category is subdivided into four groups: Anglo-Saxon family names such as Sydney, Melvin, and Murray; names taken from the map of England, including Chester and Ely; aromatic French names like Armand and Lucien; and the surnames of popular heroes, such as Sherman, Lincoln, and Lee. "The eldest son," they say, "is Abraham, then in order follow Hyman, Julius, Sydney, Leonard, and finally the élite Llewelyn."

B O Y S

ADOLPH .... Lewisohn
AUGUST .... Belmont (né Schonberg)
CARL .... Loeb
CASIMIR .... Stralem
CYRUS .... Adler
EMANUEL .... Lehman
FELIX .... Warburg
FRITZ .... Warburg
GUSTAVUS .... Speyer
HENRY .... Lehman, Seligman
HERBERT .... Lehman
HUGO .... Seligman
IGNATZ .... Steinhardt
JACOB .... Schiff
JULES .... Bache
JULIUS .... Sachs, Lewisohn
LAZARUS .... Goldman
LEOPOLD .... Cahn, Bache, Seligman
LUDWIG .... Dreyfus, Schiff
MARCUS .... Goldman
MAX .... Stettheimer
MAYER .... Lehman
MEYER .... Guggenheim, Lehman
MORITZ .... Warburg
MURRY .... Guggenheim
ORIN .... Lehman
OTTO .... Kahn
SANDER .... Goodhart
SEMON .... Bache
SIEGMUND .... Warburg
SIGMUND .... Neustadt, Lehman
SIMON .... Guggenheim
SOLOMON .... Loeb, Guggenheim

THEODORE ....Hellman
WOLF .... Goodhart

George Washington and Isaac Newton

Several of his [Joseph Seligman's] brothers had early Americanized their first names. Henry was originally Hermann, William was Wolf, James was Jacob, Jesse was Isaias, and Leopold was Lippmann. As parents, they began naming their children after the great heroes of their adopted land. Joseph's sons included George Washington Seligman . . . Isaac Newton Seligman and Alfred Lincoln Seligman—a quaint compromise. Joseph planned to call the boy Abraham Lincoln Seligman, but decided the name was too Judaic to perpetuate in America. . . . James also had a Washington and a Jefferson.

Stephen Birmingham, *Our Crowd,* Harper & Row, 1967

Before Rachel's Return

In the New York telephone directory (Winter, 1934–35), I find Cohens male named Allen, Archie, Arthur, Bert, Carl, Charles, Clarence, DeWitt, Edgar, Edward, Edwin, Elliot, Ellis, Ernest, Felix, Frank, Frederick, George, Godfrey, Harry, Harvey, Henry, Herbert, Howard, Irving, Jack, Jacques, James, Jerome, Jules, Lawrence, Lee, Lester, Malcolm, Mark, Martin, Marvin, Mathias, Maximilian, Maxwell, Michael, Mitchell, Mortimer, Morton, Murray, Norman, Oscar, Paul, Philip, Ralph, Sidney, Theodore, Victor and William, and Cohens female named Amelia, Annabel, Annette, Bessie, Betty, Birdie, Charlotte, Dorothy, Elizabeth, Emily, Estelle, Ethel, Florence, Gertrude, Helen, Irene, Jennie, Josephine, Lucille, Mae, Mary, Myra, Rae, Renee, Rose, Sophia, Sue and Sylvia. There are but three Moses Cohens, three Moes and one Moise, but there are seven Lawrences, eight Herberts and fifteen Henrys. Among the ladies there is not a single Rachel, Miriam or Rebecca, and the four surviving Sarahs are overborne by three Sadies, two Saras and one Sally.

H. L. Mencken, *The American Language* (4th edition),
Alfred A. Knopf, 1937

Artistes

Among the East Side Jews of New York (now mainly translated to the Bronx) any youth showing a talent for music is likely to abandon his original given-name for Misha, Jasha or Sasha, all of them Russian diminutives; and among the younger female intelligentsia, Sonia is a prime favorite. But these are probably only passing fashions.

H. L. Mencken, *The American Language* (4th edition), Alfred A. Knopf, 1937

Jack or Jake?

If you were born in Europe and your name was Jacob, you were automatically called "Jack." But if you were born in America and your name was Jacob, they called you "Yonkele," a Yiddish endearment meaning, "little Jacob." This . . . is the story of our people in America—the attempt of the ghetto to be Americanized, and the attempt of the Americanized to recapture the flavor of the ghetto.

Harry Golden, *Enjoy, Enjoy,* World Publishing Company, 1960

. . . . let me explain in case someone doesn't know the name Yonkel—Yonkel is the Yiddish for Jacob and Yiddish is the Jewish for Jewish—I hope that's clear, for Yonkel always said all his Gentile friends called him Yonkel and all his Jewish friends called him Jack . . .

Molly Picon, *Molly! An Autobiography,* Simon and Schuster, 1980

HEBRAICA

THE GOOD BOOK OF
NAMES

The Old Testament may be the ultimate name book for Jewish parents, listing a dizzying number (about 2,800) of personages with names ranging from the familiar—Sarah and Benjamin and Rachel and Joshua—to the more distinctive—Dinah and Keturah and Ephraim and Josiah—to the extremely unusual and the truly bizarre. Biblical names in general have enjoyed such favor over the past few decades among Jews and non-Jews alike that many of the "normal" ones—Sarah et al, as well as Adam, Jonathan, Rebecca, Daniel, and Aaron—are now in danger of being overused, while others such as Hannah and Leah, Ethan and Jacob are rapidly advancing in popularity.

Still, the Old Testament includes such a vast number of names, especially for boys, that many fresh-sounding choices remain. We've divided these into three groups. The first we think of as mainstream but distinctive—the Dinahs and Josiahs of the bunch—and some entries include the authentic Hebrew equivalents, which sound somewhat more offbeat. If you love the flavor of biblical names like Rebecca and Hannah and Benjamin but find the usual selections boring and overly familiar, consider one of the following:

MAINSTREAM BUT DISTINCTIVE

GIRLS

ABIGAIL
BETHIA
DEBORAH/
    DEVORAH
DELILAH
DINAH
ESTHER/HADASSAH
EVE/CHAVA
JAEL
JEMIMA

JUDITH/YEHUDIT
KETURAH
KEZIA(H)
MARA
MIRIAM
NAOMI
RUTH
SARAI
TAMAR
ZORAH (a place name)

BOYS

ABEL
ABNER
ABRAHAM/
    AVRAHAM
ADLAI
AMOS
ASHER

CALEB
DARIUS
ELI
ELIJAH
ELISHA
EMANUEL
ENOCH

EPHRAIM	LEVI
ESAU	MALACHI
EZEKIEL	MICAH
EZRA	MOSES/MOSHE
GABRIEL/GAVRIEL	NATHAN
GIDEON	NATHANIEL
HIRAM	NOAH
ISAAC/YITZHAK	OMAR
ISAIAH	PHINEAS/PINCHAUL
JAEL	RAPHAEL
JARED	REUBEN
JEDIDIAH	SAMSON
JEREMIAH	SAUL/SHAUL
JETHRO	SETH
JOEL	SIMEON
JONAH	SOLOMON/SHLOMO
JOSEPH/YOSEF	TOBIAS
JOSIAH	URIAH
JUDAH	ZACHARIAH
JUDE	

U N U S U A L   B U T   U S A B L E

All of the names in the second and third Old Testament groups are highly unusual; what divides them is that some seem within the realm of possibility for parents who want a unique name for their baby, while others are simply too strange even to be considered. Placing a name in the second group, the unusual-but-usables, rather than the third, was strictly a judgment call; when in doubt about a name, we put it in, figuring that parents attracted to this list would have a high tolerance for oddity. Those with more conservative tastes may want to look here for unusual variations on more familiar names—Anah, Michal, Heriah, and Mattithiah stand out—and relegate the rest to the third biblical group—names that are terminally bizarre.

If you are interested in this kind of name but find nothing quite right on this list, look through your Bible: there are lots more where these came from.

G I R L S

ABIAH	MICHAL
ADAH	MILCAH
ADINA	NAARAH
AHIJAH	ORPAH
AHINOAM	RIZPAH
AIAH	SHELOMITH
ANAH	SHIFRA
APHRAH	SHUAH
ASENATH	TAPHATH
ATARAH	TIKVAH
ATHALIAH	TIMNA
AZUBAH	TIRZAH
BAARA	YEDIDA
BATHSHEBA	ZERUIAH
BILHAH	ZILLAH
ELISHEBA/ELISHEVA	ZILPAH
EPHRATH	ZIPPORAH
HADASSAH	
HELAH	
HODESH	
HODIAH	
JEHUDIJAH	
JOCHEBED	
MAACHAH	

B O Y S

ABIDAH	HAZO
ABIEL	ISCAH
ABSALOM	ISHBAK
ADRIEL	ISSACHAR
AHBAN	JABEZ
AIAH	JACHIN
ALVAH	JAHAZIAH
AMAZIAH	JAMIN
AMRAM	JAPHETH
ARAM	JARIB
ASA	JAROAH
ASAPH	JASHUB
AZARIAH	JAVAN
AZEL	JEMUEL
BARUCH	JERAH
BENAIAH	JERED
BOAZ	JERIAH
CHESED	JEROHAM
ELEAZAR/ELIEZER	JESHUA
ELIASHIB	JETHER
ENOS	JEZOAR
EPHAH	JOAB
EPHER	JOAH
EPHRON	JOSADAK
ESHTON	JOZABAD
GAHAM	KEMUEL
GEDALISH	KENAN
GERSHOM/GERSON	LABAN
HADAR	LOTAN
HANOCH	MALCHIAH
HARAN	MALLUCH

MANASSEH	TEBAH
MATTATHAH	TEMA
MATTITHIAH	TEMAN
MEDON	TERAH
MESHULLAM	TIRAS
MIDIAN	URIJAH
NAHATH	YOAV
NETHANIAH	ZACCHUR
OBADIAH	ZEBEDEE
OZNI	ZEBEDIAH
RAPHA	ZEDEKIAH
SHEM	ZEPHANIAH
SHIMON	ZERETH

T R U L Y   B I Z A R R E

Simply being unusual and unfamiliar was not enough to get a name damned to this list: the Bible is too full of merely strange names for that. Rather, what are sequestered here are names that make you laugh out loud when you hear them, names that have unpleasant associations with other English words (Hoglah, Mishma, Asahel), names that sound native not to America or even Israel but to the planet Krypton. This selection is for your entertainment only: we do not—repeat, do *not*—want to receive any letters from parents who say they named their daughter Hazelelponi on the advice of our book.

G I R L S

AHOLIBAMAH	HOGLAH
BASHEMATH	PENINNAH
EGLAH	REUMAH
HAZELELPONI	

B O Y S

ARPHAXAD	MESHA
ASAHEL	MIBSAM
BETHUEL	MISHMA
BUKKI	MIZZAH
GATAM	NAPHISH
HACHALIAH	PELEG
HETH	PILDASH
HUR	SHOBAB
JIDLAPH	THAHASH
JOBAB	UZI
JOKTAN	ZADOK
LEUMMIM	ZEBULUN
MAGOG	ZIMRAM
MAHALALEEL	ZIMRI
MASSA	ZIPH

THE BAD BOOK OF NAMES

There are some names from the Bible that, no matter how religious or traditional you are, no matter how offbeat your tastes, you just cannot use. While Moses, Noah, Samson, and Delilah may finally be escaping their primal biblical images, other Old Testament names still carry unpleasant associations—Job, Cain, Esau, Ishmael, for example. And you still can't name your son Lot or Sheba (yes, it's a he in the Bible, as well as the Queen of), and you can't name your baby girl Sodom or Jezebel. Nor can you name your child Ichabod (Crane), Ebenezer (Scrooge), (Jumpin') Jehosephat, or Hagar (the Horrible). Gomer (Pyle) and his cousin Jobab not only live on the farm, they bought it.

If you have twins, don't be tempted to name them after the Biblical brothers Huppim and Shuppim, or Huz and Buz. Neither should you use Uz (no relation), nor Gog, Ham, Mash, Kish, or Cush. And Nun would seem to be a highly misleading name for a Jewish boy.

NEW TESTAMENT NO-NOS

Well, maybe no-no is a bit too strong. Lord knows there are legions of Mark Goodmans and Matthew Cohens on the Bar Mitzvah rolls. And we have not hesitated to include many of the names below on some of our recommended lists. Still, you might want to bear in mind the New Testament origins of the following:

G I R L S

BETHANY (a place
   name)
CANDACE
CHLOE
CLAUDIA
DORCAS
DRUSILLA
LYDIA

MARTHA
PHOEBE
PRISCILLA
RHODA
SALOME
SUSANNAH
TABITHA

B O Y S

ALEXANDER
ANDREW
BARNABAS
BARTHOLOMEW
CLEMENT
JAMES
JOHN
LINUS
LUCIUS
LUKE
MARK
MATTHEW

NATHANIEL
NICHOLAS
PAUL
PETER
PHILIP
SILAS
SIMON
STEPHEN
THADDEUS
THOMAS
TIMOTHY
TITUS

Haifa-nated names

When, after years of struggle, the State of Israel was finally established in 1948, its understandably chauvinistic citizens enthusiastically championed the revival of the Hebrew language begun by earlier Zionists, a sentiment that would be dramatically reflected in the naming of newborns. In fact, so significant was this rite considered that a Commission for Hebrew Nomenclature was established, which still exists as a division of the Ministry of the Interior. This body drew up a multivolume canon of information on individual Hebrew names, as well as rules for the Hebraization of both Yiddish and non-Jewish names.

Since there was a desire to erase the collective memory of the recent Holocaust, Germanic names were the first to go. Often literal translations were sought for Yiddish names, for instance Raizel might become Varda (both meaning "rose"), and Shayna ("beauty") might be transformed into Yaffa. The Bible was scoured for the more obscure ancient names: Rachel and Rebecca were joined—and eventually all but replaced—by Abishag and Avital. Biblical place names were also unearthed, and before long there were lots of little Kinereths and Carmelas in the kibbutz. Another source was the natural environment, in which the Sabras delighted, and many of the words for fauna (Eyal = stag) and flora (see Desert Blooms, page 72) all became popular names.

But perhaps most popular of all were the newly created names, which reflected the spirit of independence that infused the new nation. Some of these are:

G I R L S

(Note: most of the names ending with *a* can be spelled with or without an *h* at the end.)

ABIRA	BIRA
ADENA	DERORA
ADIRA	DIZA
ADIVA	DORIT
ALEEZA	ELANA
ALIYA	ELIANA
AMALIA	ELIORA
ANAT	GALI
ARELLA	GAYORA
ARIELLA	GAZIT
ASHIRA	GILI
ATALIA	GIVA
AVIVA	HADARA
AYALA	HAVIVA
AZAH	ITI

KADIA	RANANA
KELILA	RAZIA
KEREN	ROCHI
LIAN	ROEM
LIAT	RONI
LIMOR	RUTI
LIORA	SHIRA
LIRAZ	SHIRI
LIRON	SIDRA
LIRONA	SIVANA
MARGALIT	SOSHI
MIRIT	TALI
MORIAH	TALIA
NAAMIT	TALMA
NAAVA	TEMIRA
NEIMA	TOVA
NILI	YAFFA
NIRA	YARDENA
NOA	YONA
ODELIA	ZAHARA
OPHRAH/OFRA	ZEVA
ORAH	ZIONA
ORIT	ZIVA

B O Y S

ABBA	ADMON
ABIR	AITAN
ADI	AMICHAI
ADIR	AMIEL
ADIV	AMON

ARI
AVIV
AYAL
AZI
BENZI
DEROR
DORON
DOV
ETAN
GAL
GIBOR
GILI
GUR
GURI
GURIEL
HADAR
ILON
KALIL
LEOR/LIOR
LERON/LIRON
NAOR
NAVON
NIV
NOAM
NUR
NURI

OFER
ORAN
OREN
ORIN
ORLI
RAVIV
RAZ
RAZI
RAZIEL
RONEN
SAGI
SHAI
SHAMIR
SHARON
TABBAI
TAL
TAMIR
URI
YAAD
YAAL
YALON
YARON
YONATAN
ZAMIR
ZIV
ZOHAR

Desert blooms

In creating their brave new nomenclature, the Israelis have frequently turned to nature for inspiration, and many of their coinages represent the profusion of flowers, trees, and other fruits of the earth. For example:

GIRLS

ADMONIT	Peony
ALONA	Oak tree
AMIRA	Ear of grain
ARAVA	Willow
ARNA	Cedar
ARZA	Cedar beams
CARMELA	Garden
CHAMANIT	Sunflower
CHARTZIT	Chrysanthemum

CHAVATZELET ....Lily
CHELMONIT ....Crocus
DAFNE, DAFNA .... Laurel
DALIAH .... Dahlia
DALIT ....Trailing vine
EINAV .... Grape
GANA .... Garden
HADAS, HADASSAH .... Myrtle
ILANA(H) ....Tree
IRIT .... Daffodil
KALANIT .... Anemone
LEVONA ....Frankincense
LILACH ....Lilac
LUZ .... Almond tree
MARGANIT .... Pimpernel
MARVA ....Sage
NARKIS ....Narcissus
NETA ....Seedling
NETAH .... Plant
NITZAH .... Bud
NURIT .... Buttercup
ORNA(H) ....Pine
PERACH .... Flower
PERI .... Fruit
RAKEFET .... Cyclamen
RIMONA(H) ....Pomegranate
SHAKED ....Almond
SHIKMA ....Sycamore
SHITA .... Acacia
SHOSHANA .... Lily or rose
SIGLIAH .... Violet
TAMAR ....Date palm
TIDHAR .... Elm
TILTAN .... Clover
TIRZA ....Linden tree
TUT ....Strawberry
TZIPOREN .... Carnation

VARDA . . . . .Rose
VERED . . . . .Rose
YAARA . . . . Honeysuckle
YAKINTON . . . . Hyacinth
YASMIN . . . . Jasmine

B O Y S

ALON . . . . Oak tree
AMIR . . . . Treetop
ARMON . . . . .Chestnut
BAR . . . . Wheat
DEKEL . . . . .Palm tree
EILON . . . . Oak tree
ESHKOL . . . . Cluster of grapes
GAN. . . . . Garden
ILAN . . . . .Tree
KANIEL . . . . Reed or stalk
LUZ . . . . .Almond tree
MOR . . . . Myrrh
NARKIS . . . . .Narcissus
NITZAM . . . . Bud
NUFAR . . . . Water lily
OMER . . . . .Sheaf of grain
OREN . . . . .Fir tree, cedar
REICHAN . . . . .Basil
RIMON . . . . Pomegranate
TIDHAR . . . . Elm
TOMER . . . . .Date palm
TZABAR . . . . .Cactus
ZAYIT . . . . Olive tree
ZER . . . . .Wreath of flowers

SHABBAT SHALOM, SHABBAT

There are several Hebrew names that are particularly associated with certain times of the year and holidays, some symbolically, some literally. Among them are:

G I R L S

ADARA	Twelfth month in the Jewish calendar; Purim
ALONA	Tu b'Shvat
AMIRA	Shavuot
ARAVA	Sukkoth
AVIVA	Spring
AVUKA	Hannukah
ELULA	Sixth month in the Jewish calendar
ESTHER	Purim
HADASSAH	Purim

ILANA	Tu b'Shvat
KAMA	Shavuot
LEHAVA	Hannukah
LEUMA	Israeli Independence Day
LUZ	Tu b'Shvat
MEORA	Hannukah
NAOMI	Shavuot
NEILA	Yom Kippur
NERA	Hannukah
NETA	Tu b'Shvat
NIRA	Tu b'Shvat
NISSANA	First month of the Jewish calendar; Passover
RIMON	Sukkoth
SAHAR	Rosh Hodesh
TAMAR	Sukkoth
TAMMUZ	Fourth month of the Jewish calendar; spring
TSHUVA	Rosh Hashonah
UMA	Israeli Independence Day
URIELA	Hannukah
YISRAELA	Israeli Independence Day
YONA	Yom Kippur

B O Y S

ADAR	Twelfth month of the Jewish calendar; Purim
AKIVA	Lag b'Omer
ALON	Tu b'Shvat
AMIR	Shavuot
ARTZI	Israeli Independence Day
AV	Fifth month of the Jewish calendar

AVIV	Spring
BOAZ	Shavuot
CHAGAI	Any Jewish holiday
DAGAN	Shavuot
ELON	Tu b'Shvat
ELUL	Sixth month of the Jewish calendar
LUZ	Tu b'Shvat
MAOZ	Hannukah
MENACHEM	Tishah b'Av
MORDECHAI	Purim
NISSAN	First month of the Jewish calendar; Passover
OMER	Lag b'Omer
RIMON	Sukkoth
SAHAR	Rosh Hodesh
SHABAT	Sabbath
STAV	Autumn
TAMMUZ	Fourth month of the Jewish calendar; spring
URI	Hannukah
YISRAEL	Israeli Independence Day
YONA(H)	Yom Kippur

Yiddish lit I

Yiddish literature is rich in colorful names. For example, consider the following found in some of the stories of Isaac Bashevis Singer:

F E M A L E

ALIZA . . . . The Image
BASHELE . . . . The Family Moskat
BRONYA . . . . The Family Moskat
DACHA . . . . The Family Moskat
DINAH . . . . The Family Moskat
ELKA . . . . Gimpel the Fool
ELZBIETA . . . . The Magician of Lublin
FEIGELE . . . . The Family Moskat
GRENE . . . . Gimpel the Fool
GRISHA . . . . The Family Moskat

HADASSAH .... *The Family Moskat*
HALINA .... *The Magician of Lublin*
HAMA .... *The Family Moskat*
MACHLA .... *The Image*
MALKAH .... *The Image*
MASHA .... *Enemies, A Love Story; The Family Moskat*
MINNA .... *The Family Moskat*
NAMAH .... *Gimpel the Fool*
NECHA .... *The Image*
NESHA .... *The Family Moskat*
PESHA .... *Gimpel the Fool*
PUAH .... *Enemies, A Love Story*
ROISE .... *Gimpel the Fool*
SALKA .... *The Image*
SALTSHA .... *The Family Moskat*
SHEVA .... *Enemies, A Love Story*
SHIFRA .... *Gimpel the Fool*
SHOSHA .... *The Family Moskat*
SIMCHAH .... *The Family Moskat*
TAMAR .... *The Family Moskat*
TRINA .... *The Image*
TSILKA .... *The Image*
YENTEL .... *Gimpel the Fool*
YENTL .... *The Image*
ZEFTEL .... *The Magician of Lublin*
ZIREL .... *Gimpel the Fool*
ZLATEH .... *Gimpel the Fool*
ZYLKA .... *The Image*

M A L E

ABBA .... *Gimpel the Fool*
ALTER .... *The Image*

AMRAM . . . . *The Image*
ASA . . . . *The Family Moskat*
AVIGDOR . . . . *The Family Moskat*
BARUCH . . . . *The Magician of Lublin*
BERELE . . . . *The Image*
BERISH . . . . *The Magician of Lublin*
CHAIM . . . . *The Image*
CHANANIAH . . . . *Gimpel the Fool*
EBER . . . . *Gimpel the Fool*
GEDALYAH . . . . *The Family Moskat*
GERSHON . . . . *The Image*
GETZEL . . . . *The Image*
GIMPEL . . . . *Gimpel the Fool*
HASKELL . . . . *The Magician of Lublin*
HERSHEL . . . . *The Image*
HESHEL . . . . *The Family Moskat*
JERACHMIEL . . . . *The Family Moskat*
KATRIEL . . . . *Gimpel the Fool*
KOPPEL . . . . *The Family Moskat*
LEVI . . . . *The Family Moskat*
LIPPE . . . . *Gimpel the Fool*
MANYEK . . . . *The Family Moskat*
MAYER . . . . *The Image*
MENASSAH . . . . *The Family Moskat*
MENDEL . . . . *The Image*
MESHULAM . . . . *The Family Moskat*
MEYERL . . . . *The Family Moskat*
MOISHE . . . . *Gimpel the Fool*
MORDECAI . . . . *The Family Moskat*
MOSHE . . . . *The Family Moskat; The Image; Gimpel the Fool*
MOTKE . . . . *The Image*
MOTTELE . . . . *The Image*
NAHUM . . . . *The Image; Gimpel the Fool*
PESSEL . . . . *The Family Moskat*
PINNIE . . . . *The Family Moskat*
SHMUEL . . . . *The Image; Enemies, A Love Story*

TEVEL .... *The Image*
TREITEL .... *Gimpel the Fool*
WOLF .... *The Family Moskat*
YANEK .... *The Family Moskat*
YANKEL .... *The Image*
YASHA .... *The Magician of Lublin*
YEZKHEK .... *The Family Moskat*
ZADDOK .... *The Family Moskat*
ZELLIG .... *Gimpel the Fool*
ZISHE .... *Gimpel the Fool*

A MIXED MARRIAGE OF NAMES

If one of you is Jewish and the other's not, you've probably already made a lot of compromises in your relationship in order to honor both your faiths. You had both a minister and a rabbi at your wedding, you eat ham only at Easter; maybe you put a Star of David atop your Christmas tree. Now you're having a baby, and you want a name that has meaning in both your cultures, a name that's traditionally been used by both Christians and Jews. Does that mean yet another compromise? Of course—but, like the others you've made, it should be one that you both will be able to live with.

Some of the names on this list are classic Hebrew ones that have also traditionally been used by Christians: Daniel, for example, and David and Elizabeth. Others, while they may be English or French or Greek by derivation, have been well used by Jewish parents through the years. We've also included names that, though they may be a tad overused—Sarah, for example, and Benjamin and Jonathan—nonetheless offer the requisite compromise. If you don't mind choosing a name that's popular or even prefer one, then Jessica or Joshua may satisfy all your criteria. If, however, you have a horror of giving your child a trendy name, consult also So Far In They're Out on page 33, or the more far-reaching version in *Beyond Jennifer & Jason.*

Of course, not every conceivable option is on this list. Depending on your religious feeling (and also, to some extent, on your last name), you and your spouse may be comfortable giving your child a name as goyish as Margaret or as Jewish as Isaac—both perfectly sound names, but not included here. And while you may also be comfortable with a name as trendy as Tiffany or as musty as Milton, we're not, and so we've excluded options at the very extremes of the style spectrum. (If you insist on naming your child Tiffany or Milton, we don't want to take responsibility for it.)

Here, a wide selection of names that afford a good compromise for parents in mixed marriages:

G I R L S

ABIGAIL	ANNA
ADRIENNE	ANNABEL
ALEXANDRA	ANNE
ALICE	ANYA
AL(L)ISON	ARABELLA
ALLEGRA	BEATRICE
ALYSSA	BROOKE
AMBER	BRYN
AMELIA	CAMILLA
AMY	CARLY
ANDREA	CAROLINE

CELIA
CHARLOTTE
CHLOE
CLAIRE
CLARISSA
CLAUDIA
DAISY
DALE
DANA
DANIELLE
DARA
DEBORAH
DELIA
DIANA
DINAH
DORA
ELEANOR
ELIZA
ELIZABETH
ELLA
ELLEN
EMILY
EMMA
EVE
FAY
FLORA
FRANCES
GABRIELLA
GEORGIA
GILLIAN
GWYN(NE)
HANNAH
HARRIET

HELEN
HELENA
HENRIETTA
HILARY
HOPE
IMOGENE
ISABEL
IVY
JADE
JANE
JENNIFER
JENNY
JESSICA
JESSIE
JILL
JOANNA
JORDAN
JOSEPHINE
JULIA
JULIANA
JULIET
KATE
KEZIA(H)
LACEY
LARA
LARISSA
LAURA
LAUREL
LAUREN
LEIGH
LEILA
LESLIE
LIBBY

LILY	OLIVIA
LINDSAY	PHOEBE
LOUISA	POLLY
LUCY	RACHEL
LYDIA	RAMONA
LYNN	RAPHAELA
MADELINE	REBECCA
MARGO(T)	REGINA
MARIAN	RENATA
MARISSA	ROSE
MARTHA	ROWENA
MAUD	ROXANNE
MAY	SALLY
MELISSA	SAMANTHA
MEREDITH	SARA(H)
MIA	SOPHIA
MILLICENT	SOPHIE
MINNIE	STEPHANIE
MIRANDA	SUSAN
MOLLY	SUSANNAH
NANCY	TESSA
NELL	VIOLET
NESSA	WILLA
NICOLA	ZANDRA
NINA	ZARA
NORA	ZOE

B O Y S

ABBOTT	ERIC
ABNER	ETHAN
ADAM	EZRA
ADLAI	FELIX
ADRIAN	FRANK
ALEC	FRAZIER
ALEX	FREDERICK
ALEXANDER	GABRIEL
AMOS	GEORGE
ANDREW	GORDON
ASHER	GREGORY
BARNABY	HARRIS
BENJAMIN	HARRISON
BRANDON	HARRY
BRUNO	HENRY
BYRON	HOMER
CALEB	HUGO
CALVIN	JACK
CHARLES	JACOB
CLAUDE	JARED
CLAY	JASPER
COLE	JEREMIAH
CONRAD	JEREMY
DANIEL	JESSE
DAVID	JONATHAN
DAVIS	JORDAN
DEREK	JOSEPH
EDWARD	JOSHUA
ELI	JULIAN
ELIOT	JUSTIN

KYLE
LEO
LIONEL
LOREN
LOUIS/LEWIS
LOWELL
LUCAS
MALACHI/
  MALACHY
MALCOLM
MARCUS
MATTHEW
MAX
MICHAEL
MILO
NATHANIEL
NED
NOEL
OLIVER

OWEN
PAUL
PETER
PHILLIP
RAPHAEL
REED
REX
RUSSELL
SAM
SAMUEL
SETH
SIMON
SPENCER
STEPHEN
TOBIAS
TYLER
WILL
WILLIAM
ZACHARY

STAR (OF DAVID) SEARCH

REEL NAME OR REAL?

If you have any interest in naming your child in honor of a favorite Jewish celebrity, you have two options—you can be influenced by his or her real ethnic name, or by the nom de plume or de cinema, comedy, politics, whatever. Here are some possibilities, most of which date back to the pre-David Steinberg/Garry Shandling days, when it was thought that marquee names had to be short and Anglo-Saxon:

AARON	or RED	(Buttons)
ADOLPH	or HARPO	(Marx)
ALFRED	or LENNY	(Bruce)
ALLEN	or WOODY	(Allen)
ALVIN	or TONY	(Martin)
ASA	or AL	(Jolson)
AVROM	or MICHAEL	(Todd)
BELLE	or BEVERLY	(Sills)
BENNY	or JACK	(Benny)
BERNARD	or TONY	(Curtis)
BERNICE	or BEATRICE	(Arthur)

BETTY	or LAUREN	(Bacall)
BORGE	or VICTOR	(Borge)
DAVID	or DANNY	(Kaye)
ELLEN	or CASS	(Elliot)
EMANUEL	or EDWARD G.	(Robinson)
ESTHER	or ANN	(Landers)
ETTORE	or ITALO	(Svevo)
EUGENE	or MICHAEL	(Landon)
FRANCINE	or ABBE	(Lane)
GERSHON	or GARSON	(Kanin)
IRA	or JEFF	(Chandler)
IRVING	or BERT	(Lahr)
IRWIN	or ALAN	(King)
ISAIAH	or ED	(Wynn)
ISIDORE	or EDDIE	(Cantor)
ISRAEL	or IRVING	(Berlin)
ISRAEL	or LEE	(Strasberg)
ISSUR	or KIRK	(Douglas)
JACOB	or RODNEY	(Dangerfield)
JACOB	or GEORGE	(Gershwin)
JACOB	or JAN	(Peerce)
JEROME	or GENE	(Wilder)
JOSEPH	or JERRY	(Lewis)
JOYCE	or JANE	(Seymour)
JULIUS	or JOHN	(Garfield)
JULIUS	or GROUCHO	(Marx)
LEONARD	or BUDDY	(Hackett)
LEONARD	or TONY	(Randall)
MARION	or PAULETTE	(Goddard)
MARVIN	or NEIL	(Simon)
MENDEL	or MILTON	(Berle)
MILTON	or MICHAEL	(Kidd)
MILTON	or SOUPY	(Sales)
MURRAY	or JAN	(Murray)
MYRON	or MIKE	(Wallace)
NATHAN	or NAT	(Burns)
PAULINE	or ABIGAIL	(Van Buren)

ROSETTA	or PIPER	(Laurie)
SAMUEL	or ZERO	(Mostel)
SAMUEL	or TRISTAN	(Tzara)
SHIRLEY	or SHELLEY	(Winters)
SIDNEY	or STEVE	(Lawrence)
YACOV	or JACKIE	(Mason)
YITZROCH	or LARRY	(Rivers)

"Shirley Schrift isn't a very good name for an actress," she told me. "Let's see if we can figure out another one . . . What's your mother's maiden name?"

"Winter," I told her.

She wrote it down. "Do you like 'Shirley'?" she asked.

"God, no, there's millions of Shirleys all over Brooklyn, all named after Shirley Temple."

"Well, wouldn't you like a name that sounds like Shirley in case someone calls you?"

I thought for a moment. "Shelley is my favorite poet, but that's a last name, isn't it?"

She wrote it on the card in front of "Winter." She looked at it. "Not anymore it isn't. Shelley Winter. That's your name."

Shelley Winters, *Shelley Also Known as Shirley,* William Morrow and Company, 1980

MOVIE MOGUL NAMES

They're back, and parents, on the cutting edge of fashion, Jewish or not—from Susan Sarandon to Sally Field, Kevin Costner to Michael J. Fox—are using them again. They're the Movie Mogul names, and these days a Ben or a Barney is more likely to have a pacifier in his mouth than a cigar. So if you envision your boychik taking over Paramount or starting a studio of his own, you might consider these names:

ABE	Schneider
ADOLPH	Zukor
ALBERT	Warner
BARNEY	Balaban
BEN	Schulberg
BEN	Warner
CARL	Laemmle
DAVID	Selznick
HARRY	Cohn
HARRY	Warner
IRVING	Thalberg
JACK	Warner

JESSE	Lasky
JOE	Schenck
LEWIS	Selznick
LOUIS	B. Mayer
MARCUS	Loew
NICK	Schenck
SAMUEL	Goldwyn
SAMUEL	Warner
SOL	Wurtzel

A self-made man may prefer a self-made name.

—Judge Learned Hand, on granting permission for
Samuel Goldfish to change his name to Samuel Goldwyn

Sam Fox is just a few months old, but already his dad can see it coming. It'll be on the third page of *Daily Variety* or the *Hollywood Reporter* in, say, 2017. Just a single sentence in one of the gossipy columns that'll keep track of wheeling and dealing in the entertainment industry of the twenty-first century: "Sam Fox, Max Spielberg and Harry Benedek were spotted having lunch yesterday, talking about a big deal. . . ."

Michael J. Fox imagines the line and he laughs. "With my kid's name," he says, "everybody says he definitely gonna be a studio head."

Premiere

JEWISH JOCKS

(NO, IT'S NOT A CONTRADICTION IN TERMS)

Surprisingly enough, whole volumes have been written on the subject of great Jews in sports—there have been that many. Relatively few of them have been major league baseball players, although among them were such all-time greats as Sandy Koufax and Hank Greenberg. Similarly, NFL rosters have not been loaded down with Jewish names, but key players like Sid Luckman and Allie Sherman were among those who helped shape the modern game.

The playgrounds of the Lower East Side were among the cradles of basketball, and the histories of both the college game and the NBA are studded with the names of Jewish stars like Red Holzman, Dolph Shayes, and Red Auerbach. But the sport at which Jews have really excelled—since the eighteenth century when Daniel Mendoza was acknowledged as the greatest fighter in the world—is boxing. So there!

So, in the hopes of encouraging physical agility in your child, you might want to consider the names of the following athletes, some chosen for their outstanding prowess, others, we must admit, for their interesting names and nicknames:

AARON "FUZZY"
Kallet

AARON "ROSY"
Rosenberg

ABRAHAM "THE
LITTLE HEBREW"
Attell

ABRAHAM Saperstein

ADOLPH Schayes

AL Davis

AL "FLIP" Rosen

ALBERT "DER YID-
DESHER VILD-
KAT" Loeb

ALEXANDER "AL"
Schacht

ALEXANDER
"ALLIE" Sherman

ALEXANDER
"BROADWAY"
Smith

ALPHONSE Halami

ALTA "SCHOOL-
BOY" Cohen

ANDREW Cohen

ANGELA Buxton

Syracuse University end, 1907-11.

Considered greatest guard in football in early 1930s.

(b. Albert Knoehr) World featherweight champ, 1901-12.

Founder and coach, Harlem Globe-
trotters, beginning 1927.

Twelve-time NBA All-Star.

Current coach and owner, Oakland
Raiders.

Cleveland Indians infielder, first
baseman 1947-56; first man
unanimously selected for MVP.

Georgia Tech football center, 1908-
12; member Georgia Tech Hall of
Fame.

Pitcher for Washington Senators
1919-21, called "The Clown
Prince of Baseball."

Brooklyn College quarterback 1939-
42, Philadelphia Eagles 1943-47,
New York Giant coachs, 1961-64.

Major league catcher, infielder, outfielder, pitcher; 1871-1919.

World bantamweight champ, 1957-
59.

Outfielder for Brooklyn Dodgers,
Philadelphia Phillies, 1931-33.

New York Giants infielder, 1926,
1928-29.

British, won Wimbledon doubles in
1956.

ANGELICA Roseanu	(Romanian) Considered one of world's greatest woman's table tennis players in history; won Romanian women championship 17 times between 1936 and 1957.
ARNOLD "RED" Auerback	Coach of Boston Celtics, most famous coach in pro basketball history.
ART Heyman	College basketball hero of 1960s.
BARNEY Levinsky	World light heavyweight champ, 1916–20.
BARNEY "THE YID-DISH CURVER" Pelty	St. Louis Browns pitcher, 1903–12.
BARNEY Ross	(b. Barnet Rasofsky) World champion boxer, 1933–38.
BARNEY Sedran	Greatest of early basketball pros, although only 5"4.
BENJAMIN Kauff	Outfielder for New York Yankees and Giants, 1912–15.
BENJAMIN "BENNY" Leonard	World lightweight champ, 1917–25.
BENNY Friedman	Football's first great passer from 1924 to 1931.
BO (Robert) Belinsky	Pitcher for Los Angeles Angels, Philadelphia Phillies.
BRIAN Gottfried	Semifinalist at Wimbledon, 1980.
BRIAN Teacher	American tennis player, won Australian Open in 1981.
CALVIN Abrams	Major league outfielder, 1949–56.
CHARLES "BUCK-ETS" Goldenberg	University of Wisconsin football back, 1930–32; Green Bay Packers, blocking back and guard, 1933–45.
CYRIL Haas	Captain of Princeton basketball team, 1917; considered one of Princeton's all-time greats.

DANIEL Mendoza	World heavyweight champ 1891–95; father of modern scientific boxing.
DAVID "PRETZEL" Banks	Member of original Boston Celtics basketball team, 1925–29.
ELIAS Hart	First Columbia University basketball captain, 1904–05.
ELIJAH Crabbe	British boxer; had his first bout, 1788.
ERSKINE "SCISSORS" Mayer	Pitcher for Philadelphia Phillies, Chicago White Sox, 1912–19.
GEORGE "SILENT GEORGE" Stone	1906 American League batting champ playing for St. Louis Browns.
GYOZO VICTOR Barna	Hungarian table tennis ace, played from 1925–1954.
HAROLD Abrahams	English sprinter, won 100-meter dash in 1924 Paris Olympics; subject of *Chariots of Fire.*
HARRY "THE HUMAN HAIRPIN" Harris	World bantamweight champ, 1901–02.
HENRY "HAMMERIN' HANK" Greenberg	One of baseball's greatest right-handed hitters, primarily for Detroit Tigers (1933–47).
HENRY Wittenberg	Won 400 consecutive amateur wrestling matches between 1938 and 1952.
HERBERT Flam	First Jewish tennis player to reach finals of US Nationals, Forest Hills, 1950.
HERMAN Barron	Great Jewish golfer of 1930s and 1940s.
HERMAN "HAM" Iburg	Philadelphia Phillies pitcher 1902; known as the slowest pitcher ever seen in the majors.

HUGO Friend — Won Olympic bronze medal for long jump, 1906.

IRA "GENTLEMAN STREUSAND" Streusand — CCNY basketball team, 1907–09; then pro, responsible for rule requiring each player to shoot his own fouls.

IRENA Kirszenstein-Szewinska — Polish track-and-field star, considered one of greatest female track-and-field stars of all time. Won three Olympic medals in 1964.

IRVING Jaffee — Olympic speed skater, 1932.

ISAAC "IKE" Berger — Olympic weight lifter, 1956, 1960, 1964.

ISRAEL Levene — University of Pennsylvania football end, 1905–06.

JACKIE Fields — (b. Jacob Finklestein) Boxer, youngest athlete to win an Olympic gold medal, world welterweight champ, 1929–30, 1932–33.

JACOB "JACOB THE SILENT" Pincus — Considered the best American jockey in the 1850s.

JAMES Jacobs — One of the world's greatest handball players; captured first world four-wall singles title in 1964.

JENO Fuchs — Olympic fencer, 1908, 1912.

JOE "THE PRIDE OF THE GHETTO" Bernstein — Legendary early featherweight boxer, turned pro in 1894.

JOE "CHRYSANTHE-MUM JOE" Choyski — Boxer, fought Corbett, Jeffries, and Sullivan, boxed from 1889 to 1904.

JOHN Kling — One of major league baseball's greatest catchers, 1900–1913

JULIE Heldman — Second-ranked US woman tennis player, 1968, 1969.

KENNETH Holtzman — American League pitcher, 1966–79.

LAWRENCE "LON" Myers	Considered greatest 19th-century runner; held every American record from 50-yards to one mile.
LEACH Cross	(b. Louis Wallach) Lightweight boxer, from 1906–1921.
LEO Cantor	UCLA football halfback, 1938–40.
LEW Tendler	Called greatest southpaw in ring history; turned pro in 1913.
LILLIAN Copeland	Olympic track-and-field star, 1928, 1932.
LIONEL Malamed	CCNY basketball player, 1946–48; MVP in 1948 East-West Game.
LIPMAN "LIP" Pike	Baseball's first pro player, 1845–1893; also earliest known Jewish track champ.
LOUIS "LULU" Bender	Led Ivy League basketball in scoring, 1930–31.
LOUIS "THE KID" Kaplan	World featherweight boxing champ, 1925–27.
MACLYN Baker	Only Jewish basketball player ever selected for both collegiate All-American and AAU All-American honors.
MARGARETHE "GRETEL" Bergmann	German high jumper, forced off 1936 Olympics team by the Nazis.
MARK Spitz	Swimmer, first person in Olympic history to win seven gold medals in a single sport, 1972.
MARSHALL "BIGGIE" Goldberg	All-Pro defensive football player, 1946–48.
MAURI Rose	Auto racer, three-time winner of the Indianapolis 500 (1941, 1947, 1948).
MAX "MARTY" Friedman	Basketball pioneer, one of the renowned "Heavenly Twins," starting in 1914.

MAXIE Rosenbloom	World light heavyweight champ, 1930–34.
MONTE "THE NOB HILL TERROR" Attell	American bantamweight champ, 1909–10.
MONTGOMERY "MOE" Herscovitz	Olympic middleweight bronze medalist, 1920.
MORDECAI Starobin	Syracuse University tackle, 1922–24.
MORRIS "MOE" Berg	Major league Catcher, infielder, coach, 1923–39; graduate of Princeton, the Sorbonne, and Columbia Law School; later a U.S. counterintelligence agent.
MOSES Epstein	In 1870 became first Jew to play intercollegiate football.
MOSES "HICKORY" Solomon	New York Giants infielder, 1923; sometimes called "The Rabbi of Swat."
MUSHY Callahan	(b. Vicente Morris Sheer) World welterweight boxing champ, 1926–30.
NAT "MR. BASKETBALL" Holman	Member of original Boston Celtics; CCNY coach, 1920–60.
NATHANIEL "NAT" Fleisher	A major pioneer of modern boxing, founder of *Ring Magazine*.
PAUL "TWISTER" Steinberg	First known Jewish pro basketball player (1900); pro football player.
PHILIP "FISHY" Rabin	Led American Basketball League in scoring, 1937–38.
RANDY "THE RABBI" Grossman	Outstanding contemporary receiver for the Pittsburgh Steelers.
RENE Dreyfus	1938 French auto racing champ, won ten Grand Prix.
REUBEN "THE JEWEL OF THE GHETTO" Goldstein	Lightweight boxer (1925–37) and referee.

RICHARD Savitt	Wimbledon singles champ, 1951.
ROGER Ginsberg	First amateur to win Westchester Golf Open, 1962.
RONALD Blumberg	Major leaguer for eight years; baseball's number-one draft pick in 1967.
RONALD Jacobson	Earliest known Jewish pro football player, beginning 1889.
RONALD Mix	Contemporary offensive lineman for San Diego Chargers; second AFL player to be admitted to Pro Football Hall of Fame.
RONALD Mosberg	Olympic champion boxer, 1920.
SANFORD "SANDY" Koufax	Pitcher, Brooklyn and LA Dodgers, 1955–64; 1963 National League MVP; youngest player ever admitted to Baseball Hall of Fame.
SAUL Rogovin	Pitcher, led American League in earned runs average, 1951; playing for Detroit Tigers and Chicago White Sox.
SHLOMO Glickstein	High-ranking Israeli tennis player.
SIDNEY Franklin	Bullfighter; became full matador in 1945.
SIDNEY Gordon	Major league outfielder, infielder, first baseman, 1941–55.
SIDNEY Luckman	Quarterback, had brilliant twelve-year pro career; considered game's greatest long-run passer, 1939–50.
SIGMUND Harris	University of Minnesota quarterback, 1901.
STEVE Stone	Baltimore Orioles pitcher; won 1980 Cy Young award as best pitcher in American League.
TED "THE ALDGATE SPHINX" Lewis	(b. Gershon Mendeloff) World welterweight champ, 1915.

VICTOR Hershkowitz — Rated best all-round handball player in history, dominating the sport from 1947.

WILLIAM "RED" Holzman — CCNY basketball team, 1941–43; pro player for Rochester, 1946–57; renowned New York Knicks coach.

WOOLF Barnato — British auto racer, won three straight Le Mans 24-hour Grand Prix, 1928–30.

INDEX

GIRLS' NAMES

Abbe, 94
Abiah, 62
Abigail, 11, 60, 86, 94
Abira, 69
Abishag, 69
Abra, 11
Adah, 62
Adara, 75
Adelheid, 48
Adena, 69
Adina, 11, 62
Adira, 69
Adiva, 69
Admonit, 72
Adrienne, 11, 86
Ahijah, 62
Ahinoam, 62
Aholibamah, 65
Aiah, 62, 63
Al(l)ison, 86
Aleeza, 69
Alexa, 11
Alexis, 34
Alice, 11, 36, 48, 86
Alison, 34
Aliya, 69
Aliza, 11, 78
Allegra, 11, 86
Alona, 72, 75
Alva, 49
Alyssa, 34, 36, 86
Amalia, 69
Amanda, 34
Amber, 34, 86
Amelia, 11, 53, 86
Amira, 72, 75
Amy, 34, 86
Anah, 62
Anat, 69
Andrea, 11, 86
Angela, 99
Angelica, 100
Anita, 30
Anita, 44
Ann, 30, 94
Anna, 11, 30, 38, 86
Annabel, 11, 53, 86
Anne, 11, 86
Annette, 53
Annie, 30
Anshel, 42
Anya, 86
Aphrah, 62

Arabella, 11, 86
Aram, 63
Arava, 72, 75
Arella, 36, 69
Ariel, 34, 36
Ariella, 11, 69
Arlene, 44
Arna, 72
Arza, 72
Asenath, 62
Ashira, 69
Ashley, 34
Atalia, 69
Atarah, 62
Athaliah, 62
Audrey, 44
Augusta, 11, 49
Avital, 69
Aviva, 11, 69, 75
Avuka, 75
Ayala, 69
Azah, 69
Azubah, 62

Baara, 62
Babet, 49
Babette, 49
Baila, 42
Baile, 42
Barbara, 44
Bashele, 78
Bashemath, 65
Bathsheba, 62
Bayla, 42
Bea, 40
Beatrice, 12, 86, 93
Beatrix, 12
Becky, 40
Bella, 40
Belle, 40, 93
Bernice, 44, 46, 93
Bertha, 46, 49
Bess, 12, 40, 43
Bessie, 53
Bethany, 67
Bethia, 60
Betty, 53, 94
Beverly, 93
Bilhah, 62
Bira, 69
Birdie, 40, 53
Blanche, 40
Bluma, 42

Bonnie, 44
Bosha, 42
Brenda, 44
Brittany, 34
Bronya, 78
Brooke, 34, 86
Bryn, 86

Camilla, 12, 86
Candace, 67
Carly, 34, 86
Carmel(a), 12, 69, 72
Carol, 30, 44
Carola, 49
Caroline, 12, 31, 86
Carrie, 30
Cass, 94
Cecile, 49
Ceil, 40
Celia, 12, 87
Chaia, 42
Chamanit, 72
Charlotte, 12, 49, 53, 87
Chartzit, 72
Chava, 60
Chavatzelet, 73
Chelmonit, 73
Chelsea, 43
Cheryl, 44
Chloe, 12, 67, 87
Christina, 28
Cindy, 44
Claire, 12, 30, 87
Clara, 30, 40, 49
Clarissa, 12, 87
Claudia, 12, 67, 87
Clea, 12
Cora, 41
Courtney, 34

Dacha, 78
Dafna, 73
Dafne, 73
Dahlia, 12
Daisy, 12, 87
Dakota, 30
Dale, 12, 87
Daliah, 73
Dalit, 73
Dana, 12, 87
Danielle, 34, 37, 87
Dara, 87
Daria, 12

Davida, 12
Dawn, 44
Debby, 30, 44
Deborah, 12, 60, 87
Delia, 12, 87
Delilah, 12, 37, 60, 66
Derora, 69
Devora, 42
Devorah, 12, 60
Diana, 12, 87
Diane, 30, 44
Diantha, 12
Dinah, 12, 59, 60, 78, 87
Diza, 69
Dora, 12, 30, 41, 87
Dorcas, 67
Dorian, 12
Dorit, 69
Dorothea, 12
Dorothy, 30, 53
Drusilla, 67
Dvora, 42, 49

Eda, 49
Eden, 13
Edith, 13
Edithe, 49
Edna, 46
Eglah, 65
Eileen, 44
Einav, 73
Elaine, 44
Elana, 13, 69
Eleanor, 13, 87
Elena, 49
Eliana, 13, 69
Elicia, 34
Eliora, 13, 69
Elise, 44
Elisheba, 62
Elisheva, 62
Eliza, 13, 87
Elizabeth, 11, 13, 38, 53, 85, 87
Elka, 42, 78
Ella, 13, 87
Ellen, 87, 94
Eloise, 13
Elula, 75
Elzbieta, 78
Emanie, 49
Emanuela, 13
Emily, 13, 38, 53, 87
Emma, 13, 49, 87
Ephrath, 62
Erica, 34
Estelle, 53
Esther, 5, 41, 60, 75, 94
Ethel, 46, 53
Etta, 41
Eva, 41
Eve, 4, 13, 60, 87
Evelyn, 44

Fanny, 41
Fay, 13, 41, 87
Feigele, 78
Felicia, 49

Feya, 42
Feyga, 42
Flora, 13, 87
Florence, 53
Florette, 49
Florine, 49
Frances, 13, 87
Francesca, 10
Francine, 44, 94
Frayda, 42
Frieda, 46, 49

Gabriella, 13, 87
Gabrielle, 37
Gail, 44
Gali, 69
Gana, 73
Gayora, 69
Gazit, 69
Geneva, 13
Georgia, 13, 87
Georgina, 13
Gertrude, 46, 53
Gili, 69, 71
Gillian, 13, 87
Gita, 42
Gittel, 42
Giva, 69
Golda, 42, 46
Goldie, 41
Grene, 78
Grisha, 78
Gussie, 46
Guta, 49
Gwyn(ne), 87

Hadara, 69
Hadas, 73
Hadassah, 60, 62, 73, 75, 79
Halina, 79
Hama, 79
Hannah, 4, 13, 36, 59, 60, 87
Harriet, 13, 87
Haviva, 69
Hazelelponi, 64, 65
Heather, 11, 34
Heidi, 44
Helah, 62
Helen, 13, 53, 87
Helena, 13, 87
Helene, 44, 49
Henrietta, 13, 87
Heriah, 62
Hester, 46
Hilary, 13, 87
Hinda, 42
Hodesh, 62
Hodiah, 62
Hoglah, 64, 65
Hope, 13, 87

Ida, 41
Ilana(h), 14, 73, 76
Ilissa, 34
Imogene, 14, 87
Irena, 102
Irene, 53

Irit, 73
Irma, 46
Isabel, 14, 87
Isabella, 14
Isadora, 14
Iti, 69
Ivy, 14, 87

Jacoba, 14
Jade, 14, 87
Jael, 14, 60, 61
Jamie, 33
Jane, 14, 38, 87, 94
Janet, 44
Janice, 30, 44
Jasmine, 14
Jean, 30
Jehudijah, 62
Jemima, 60
Jemina, 14
Jenna, 14, 30
Jennie, 53
Jennifer, 30, 34, 87
Jenny, 30, 34, 87
Jessa, 14, 35, 52
Jessica, 11, 34, 86, 87
Jessie, 34, 40, 43, 87
Jezebel, 66
Jill, 44, 87
Joan, 44
Joanna, 14, 87
Joanne, 44
Jocelyn, 14
Jochebed, 62
Jody, 44
Jordan, 21, 34, 87, 89
Josepha, 14
Josephine, 14, 53, 87
Joy, 44
Joyce, 44, 94
Judith, 14, 60
Judy, 44
Julia, 14, 87
Juliana, 14, 87
Julie, 102
Juliet, 14, 87

Kadia, 70
Kaila, 14, 31
Kalanit, 73
Kama, 76
Karen, 44
Kate, 14, 31, 38, 87
Kayla, 14, 34, 42, 43
Kelila, 14, 70
Kelly, 10
Keren, 70
Ketura(h), 14, 59, 60
Kezia(h), 14, 60, 87
Kinereth, 69
Kirsten, 10
Kreindel, 42
Kyle, 11, 90

Lacey, 15, 87
Laila, 15, 42
Lara, 87

Larissa, 15, 87
Laura, 11, 15, 38, 87
Laurel, 15, 87
Lauren, 34, 87, 94
Layla, 15
Leah, 15, 59
Lee, 50, 53, 94
Lehava, 76
Leigh, 15, 87
Leila, 15, 87
Lenore, 44
Leonora, 15
Leonore, 44, 49
Leora, 15
Leslie, 44, 87
Letty, 41
Leuma, 76
Levona, 73
Leya, 42
Lian, 70
Liana, 15
Liat, 70
Liba, 42
Libby, 15, 41, 87
Lila, 15
Lilach, 73
Lillian, 30, 103
Lillie, 30
Lily, 15, 30, 41, 88
Limor, 70
Lina, 49
Linda, 30, 44
Lindsay, 34, 88
Liora, 70
Liraz, 70
Lirona, 70
Lisa, 44
Lois, 44
Loren, 35, 90
Loretta, 44
Lori, 30, 44
Lorraine, 44
Lottie, 41
Louisa, 15, 88
Louise, 15, 49
Lucille, 53
Lucius, 67
Luz, 73, 74, 76, 77
Lydia, 15, 67, 88
Lynn, 44, 88

Maachah, 62
Machla, 79
Madeline, 15, 88
Mae, 53
Maisie, 15
Malkah, 79
Mara(h), 15, 37, 60
Marcia, 44
Marcy, 30, 44
Margalit, 70
Marganit, 73
Margaret, 86
Margarethe, 103
Margot, 15
Mariah, 15
Marian, 15, 30, 88

Marilyn, 28, 44
Marion, 94
Marissa, 15, 88
Marjorie, 44
Marlene, 44
Marsha, 30
Martha, 11, 15, 67, 88
Martin, 45, 53
Marva, 73
Mary, 53
Masha, 79
Matilda, 11, 15
Mattithiah, 62, 64
Maud, 15, 88
Maxie, 104
Maxine, 44
May, 88
Melissa, 34, 88
Meora, 76
Meredith, 15, 88
Mia, 15, 88
Michaela, 15
Michal, 15, 62
Michelle, 34
Milcah, 62
Mildred, 46
Millicent, 15, 88
Millie, 41
Min, 41
Mindy, 44
Minna, 79
Minnie, 15, 88
Mirabel, 15
Miranda, 15, 88
Miriam, 11, 15, 37, 41, 53, 60
Mirit, 70
Molka, 42
Molly, 11, 15, 30, 43, 88
Mona, 44
Moriah, 15, 70
Muriel, 44
Myra, 53
Myrna, 46

Naamit, 70
Naarah, 62
Naava, 70
Nadia, 16
Nadine, 44
Nadya, 16
Namah, 79
Nancy, 30, 44, 88
Nanette, 44
Naomi, 16, 36, 60, 76
Narkis, 73, 74
Natalie, 41
Natasha, 16
Necha, 79
Neila, 76
Neima, 70
Nell, 16, 30, 88
Nellie, 30
Nera, 76
Nesha, 79
Nessa, 16, 88
Nesya, 42
Neta, 73, 76

Netah, 73
Nettie, 41
Nicola, 16, 88
Nicole, 30
Nili, 70
Nina, 16, 88
Nira, 70, 76
Nissana, 76
Nitzah, 73
Niva, 49
Noemi, 16
Nora, 88
Norma, 30, 44
Nurit, 73

Odelia, 16, 70
Odessa, 16
Ofra, 70
Olivia, 16, 88
Ophrah, 70
Orah, 70
Orit, 70
Orna(h), 73
Orpah, 62
Ozni, 64

Paula, 44
Paulette, 94
Pauline, 16, 49, 94
Pearl, 16, 41
Peninnah, 65
Perach, 73
Peri, 73
Perry, 16
Pesha, 79
Phoebe, 16, 67, 88
Phyllis, 44
Piper, 95
Polly, 16, 88
Priscilla, 67
Puah, 79

Quintana, 16
Quintina, 16

Rachel, 4, 11, 30, 33, 36, 37, 38,
   53, 59, 68, 88
Rae, 17, 53
Raisa, 17
Raizel, 42, 68
Rakefet, 73
Ramona, 17, 88
Ranana, 70
Randi, 30, 44
Raphaela, 17, 37, 88
Rayna, 17, 42
Razia, 70
Rebecca, 4, 8, 17, 33, 36, 37, 38,
   53, 59, 60, 68, 88
Regina, 49, 88
Regine, 49
Renata, 17, 49
Renee, 30, 53
Reumah, 65
Rhea, 17
Rhoda, 30, 44, 67
Rhonda, 44

Ricki, 30, 33, 44
Rimona(h), 73
Rina, 17
Rita, 45
Rivka, 42
Rizpah, 62
Roberta, 45
Rochelle, 30
Rochi, 70
Roem, 70
Roise, 79
Rosa, 17, 49
Rosalie, 45, 49
Rose, 17, 30, 41, 53, 88
Rosetta, 95
Rosie, 30
Rosina, 49
Roslyn, 45
Rowena, 17, 88
Roxanne, 17, 88
Ruby, 17
Ruth, 17, 30, 37, 60
Ruti, 70

Sabra, 17, 69
Sabrina, 17
Sacha, 17
Sadie, 30, 37, 41, 53
Sahar, 76, 77
Salka, 79
Sally, 17, 53, 88
Salome, 67
Saltsha, 79
Samantha, 30, 34, 88
Sandra, 45
Sandy, 98
Sara(h), 4, 11, 30, 33, 36, 37, 38, 53, 59, 85, 88
Sarai, 4, 17, 37, 60
Sarajane, 36
Selena, 17
Selma, 30, 47
Serena, 17
Shana, 17
Shari, 33
Sharon, 30, 45, 71
Shayna, 42
Sheila, 30, 45
Shelley, 95
Shelly, 30
Shelomith, 62
Sherry, 30, 45
Sheva, 79
Shifra, 62, 79

Shikma, 73
Shira, 70
Shiri, 70
Shirley, 28, 30, 47, 95
Shita, 73
Shosha, 79
Shoshana, 17, 73
Shuah, 62
Sibyl, 47
Sidra, 70
Sigliah, 73
Simchah, 79
Simone, 17
Sivana, 70
Sodom, 66
Sonia, 17, 54
Sophia, 17, 30, 49, 53, 88
Sophie, 17, 30, 33, 41, 49, 88
Sorali, 42
Sorke, 42
Soshi, 70
Stacy, 30
Stella, 17
Stephanie, 34, 88
Sue, 53
Sura, 42
Susan, 30, 45, 88
Susannah, 17, 67, 88
Suzanne, 45
Sydney, 17, 50
Sylvia, 30, 45, 53

Tabitha, 67
Tali, 70
Talia, 17, 70
Talma, 70
Tama, 49
Tamar, 17, 60, 73, 76, 79
Tamara, 17
Tammuz, 76, 77
Taphath, 62
Temira, 70
Tess, 41
Tessa, 88
Thea, 17
Therese, 49
Tidhar, 73, 74
Tiffany, 11, 34, 86
Tikvah, 62
Tillie, 17, 41
Tiltan, 73
Timna, 62
Tirza, 73
Tirzah, 62

Tova, 17, 70
Trestel, 42
Trina, 79
Tshuva, 76
Tsilka, 79
Tut, 73
Tyne, 17
Tziporen, 73
Tzirel, 42

Uma, 76
Uriela, 76

Varda, 68, 74
Venetia, 18
Vered, 74
Viola, 18
Violet, 18, 88

Wendy, 45
Willa, 18, 88
Winona, 18

Yaara, 74
Yael, 18
Yaffa, 68, 70
Yakinton, 74
Yardena, 70
Yasmin, 74
Yedida, 62
Yehudit, 60
Yentel, 42, 79
Yentl, 79
Yetta, 47
Yisraela, 76
Yona(h), 70, 76, 77

Zahara, 70
Zandra, 88
Zara, 18, 88
Zelde, 42
Zelia, 18
Zeruiah, 62
Zeva, 70
Zia, 18
Zillah, 62
Zilpah, 62
Ziona, 18, 70
Zipporah, 62
Ziva, 70
Zoe, 18, 88
Zora, 18
Zorah, 60
Zylka, 79

INDEX

BOYS' NAMES

Aaron, 18, 30, 37, 59, 93, 99
Abba, 70, 79
Abbott, 89
Abe, 18, 30, 37, 41
Abel, 4, 18, 37, 60
Abidah, 63
Abiel, 63
Abir, 70
Abner, 18, 37, 60, 89
Abraham, 3, 4, 18, 50, 60, 99
Abram, 4, 18
Absalom, 63
Adam, 4, 30, 35, 37, 59, 89
Adar, 76
Adi, 70
Adir, 70
Adiv, 70
Adlai, 19, 60, 89
Admon, 70
Adolph, 51, 93, 99
Adrian, 19, 89
Adriel, 63
Ahban, 63
Aiah, 62, 63
Aitan, 70
Akiva, 76
Al, 93, 99
Alan, 30, 45, 94
Albert, 99
Alec, 19, 89
Alex, 89
Alexander, 34, 35, 67, 86, 89, 99
Alfred, 93
Allen, 53, 93
Allie, 98
Alon, 74, 76
Alphonse, 99
Alta, 99
Alte, 8
Alter, 79
Alvah, 63
Alvin, 47, 93
Amaziah, 63
Amichai, 70
Amiel, 70
Amir, 74, 76
Amon, 70
Amory, 19
Amos, 19, 60, 89
Amram, 63, 80
Andrew, 19, 39, 67, 89, 99
Archie, 53
Ari, 19, 71

Armand, 50
Armon, 74
Arno, 19
Arnold, 47, 100
Arphaxad, 65
Art, 100
Arthur, 30, 53
Artzi, 76
Asa, 19, 63, 00, 93
Asahel, 64, 65
Asaph, 63
Asher, 19, 60, 89
August, 51
Av, 76
Avery, 19
Avigdor, 80
Aviv, 71, 77
Avraham, 3, 60
Avrom, 93
Avrum, 3, 42
Ayal, 71
Aza, 19
Azariah, 63
Azel, 63
Azi, 71

Bar, 74
Barnabas, 67
Barnaby, 89
Barney, 41, 100
Barry, 30, 45
Bartholomew, 67
Baruch, 63, 80
Ben, 30, 35
Benaiah, 63
Benjamin, 4, 30, 35, 37, 59, 60, 85, 89, 100
Benno, 19, 37
Benny, 93, 100
Benzi, 71
Berele, 80
Berish, 80
Bernard, 30, 47, 93
Bernie, 32
Bert, 53, 94
Bertram, 47
Bethuel, 65
Bo, 100
Boaz, 19, 63, 77
Borge, 94
Bram, 19
Brandon, 35, 89
Brendan, 30

Brian, 100
Bruce, 45
Bruno, 19, 89
Buddy, 94
Bukki, 65
Buz, 66
Byron, 19, 89

Cain, 4, 66
Caleb, 19, 37, 60, 89
Calvin, 19, 89, 100
Carl, 51, 53
Casimir, 51
Caspar, 19
Chagai, 77
Chaim, 19, 42, 80
Chananiah, 80
Charles, 19, 39, 53, 89, 100
Chayim, 8
Chesed, 63
Chester, 50
Clarence, 53
Claude, 19, 89
Clay, 89
Clement, 67
Cole, 19, 89
Conrad, 19, 89
Cush, 66
Cyril, 100
Cyrus, 51

Dagan, 77
Daniel, 11, 19, 36, 37, 39, 59, 85, 89, 98, 101
Danny, 94
Darius, 19, 37, 60
David, 4, 11, 19, 36, 37, 39, 85, 89, 94, 101
Davis, 19, 89
Dekel, 74
Derek, 19, 89
Deror, 71
DeWitt, 53
Dolph, 98
Donald, 45
Doron, 71
Dov, 19, 71
Dovid, 42
Duncan, 10
Dustin, 35

Ebenezer, 66
Eber, 80

Ed, 94
Eddie, 94
Edgar, 53
Edward 20, 53, 89, 94
Edwin, 53
Eilon, 74
Eleazar, 63
Eli, 20, 41, 60, 89
Elias, 101
Eliashib, 63
Eliezer, 63
Elijah, 20, 60, 101
Eliot, 45, 89
Elisha, 20, 60
Elliot, 53
Ellis, 53
Elon, 77
Elul, 77
Ely, 50
Emanuel, 20, 50, 51, 60, 94
Emmett, 20
Enoch, 20, 60
Enos, 63
Ephah, 63
Epher, 63
Ephraim, 20, 59, 61
Ephron, 63
Eric, 35, 89
Ernest, 53
Erskine, 101
Esau, 20, 61, 66
Eshkol, 74
Eshton, 63
Etan, 71
Ethan, 20, 59, 89
Ettore, 94
Eugene, 45, 94
Ezekiel, 20, 61
Ezra, 20, 61, 89

Felix, 20, 51, 53, 89
Frank, 20, 53, 89
Frazier, 20, 89
Frederick, 20, 53, 89
Fritz, 51

Gabriel, 20, 61, 89
Gaham, 63
Gal, 71
Gan, 74
Garson, 20, 94
Gary, 45
Gatam, 65
Gavriel, 61
Gedalish, 63
Gedalyah, 80
Gene, 45, 94
George, 20, 53, 89, 94, 101
Gershom, 63
Gershon, 80, 94
Gerson, 63
Getzel, 80
Gibor, 71
Gideon, 20, 37, 61
Gilbert, 45
Gimpel, 80
Godfrey, 53

Gog, 66
Gomer, 66
Gordon, 20, 89
Gregory, 89
Groucho, 94
Gur, 71
Guri, 71
Guriel, 71
Gus, 20, 37, 41, 50
Gustavus, 51
Gyozo, 101

Hachaliah, 65
Hadar, 63, 71
Hagar, 66
Ham, 66
Hank, 98
Hanoch, 63
Haran, 63
Harold, 32, 101
Harpo, 93
Harris, 20, 30, 89
Harrison, 20, 30, 89
Harry, 20, 30, 41, 53, 89, 101
Harvey, 32, 47, 53
Haskel, 42
Haskell, 80
Hazo, 63
Henriette, 49
Henry, 20, 30, 39, 51, 52, 53, 89, 101
Herbert, 47, 51, 53, 101
Herman, 47, 101
Hermann, 52
Hersh, 42
Hershel, 47, 80
Heshel, 80
Heth, 65
Hiram, 20, 61
Homer, 20, 89
Hosea, 20
Howard, 45, 53
Hugo, 51, 89, 102
Huppim, 66
Hur, 65
Huz, 66
Hy, 41
Hyman, 47, 50

Ian, 30
Ichabod, 66
Ignatz, 51
Ilan, 74
Ilon, 71
Ira, 30, 45, 94, 102
Irving, 28, 30, 40, 47, 53, 94, 102
Irwin, 28, 32, 47, 94
Isaac, 8, 21, 30, 41, 61, 86, 102
Isaiah, 21, 61, 94
Isaias, 52
Iscah, 63
Ishbak, 63
Ishmael, 21, 66
Isidore, 3, 28, 41, 94
Israel, 21, 41, 94, 102
Issachar, 63
Issur, 94

Italo, 94
Itzak, 28, 42
Itzik, 42

Jabez, 21, 63
Jachin, 63
Jack, 21, 41, 53, 89, 93
Jackie, 95, 102
Jacob, 35, 37, 51, 52, 54, 59, 89, 94, 102
Jacques, 53
Jahaziah, 63
Jake, 30, 33, 35, 37, 40
James, 52, 53, 67, 102
Jamin, 63
Jan, 94
Japheth, 63
Jared, 21, 37, 61, 89
Jarib, 63
Jaroah, 63
Jasha, 54
Jashub, 63
Jason, 11, 30, 35
Jasper, 21, 89
Javan, 63
Jay, 30, 45
Jedidiah, 21, 61
Jeff, 94
Jeffrey, 45
Jehosephat, 66
Jemuel, 63
Jeno, 102
Jerachmiel, 80
Jerah, 63
Jered, 63
Jeremiah, 21, 37, 61, 89
Jeremy, 35, 36, 37, 89
Jeriah, 63
Jeroham, 63
Jerome, 30, 53, 94
Jerry, 94
Jeshua, 63
Jesse, 33, 89, 97
Jether, 63
Jethro, 21, 37, 61
Jezoar, 63
Jidlaph, 65
Joab, 63
Joachim, 21
Joah, 63
Job, 66
Jobab, 65, 66
Joe, 97, 102
Joel, 45, 61
John, 67, 94, 102
Joktan, 65
Jonah, 21, 61
Jonas, 37
Jonathan, 33, 35, 37, 59, 85, 89
Jordan, 21, 34, 87, 89
Josadak, 63
Joseph, 3, 21, 61, 89, 94
Joshua, 4, 33, 35, 36, 37, 59, 86, 89
Josiah, 21, 37, 59, 61
Judah, 61
Jude, 61

Jules, 51, 53
Julian, 21, 89
Julius, 47, 50, 51, 94
Justin, 35, 89

Kalil, 71
Kalman, 21, 41
Kaniel, 74
Katriel, 80
Kelly, 10
Kemuel, 63
Kenan, 63
Kenneth, 45, 102
Kermit, 21
Kirk, 94
Kish, 66
Koppel, 80
Kyle, 11, 90

Laban, 21, 63
Labe, 42
Larry, 95
Lawrence, 45, 53, 103
Lazar, 42
Lazarus, 51
Leach, 103
Lee, 50, 53, 94
Leib, 42
Lemuel, 21, 37
Lenny, 93
Leo, 21, 41, 90, 103
Leonard, 50, 94
Leopold, 51, 52
Leor, 71
Leron, 71
Leslie, 44, 87
Lester, 47, 53
Leummim, 65
Lev, 21
Levi, 21, 61, 80
Lew, 103
Lewis, 21, 90, 97
Lincoln, 50
Linus, 67
Lionel, 21, 90, 103
Lior, 71
Lipman, 103
Lippe, 80
Lippmann, 52
Liron, 70, 71
Llewelyn, 50
Lot, 66
Lotan, 63
Lou, 41
Louis, 21, 90, 97, 103
Lowell, 21, 90
Lucas, 90
Lucien, 50
Lucy, 15, 88
Ludwig, 51
Luke, 67

Mack, 41
Maclyn, 103
Magog, 65
Mahalaleel, 65
Malachi, 22, 61, 90

Malachy, 90
Malchiah, 63
Malcolm, 22, 53, 90
Malluch, 63
Manasseh, 64
Manny, 47
Manyek, 80
Maoz, 77
Marcus, 22, 51, 90, 97
Mark, 45, 53, 66, 67, 103
Marshall, 45, 103
Marvin, 3, 28, 30, 47, 53, 94
Mash, 66
Massa, 65
Mathias, 53
Mattathah, 64
Matthew, 22, 37, 39, 66, 67, 90
Matthias, 22
Mauri, 103
Maurice, 47
Max, 11, 29, 30, 33, 34, 35, 37,
    40, 50, 51, 90, 103
Maximillian, 53
Maxwell, 53
Mayer, 42, 51, 80
Medon, 64
Melvin, 29, 47, 50
Menachem, 77
Menassah, 80
Mendel, 42, 47, 80, 94
Mesha, 65
Meshulam, 80
Meshullam, 64
Meyer, 41, 51
Meyerl, 80
Mibsam, 65
Micah, 22, 37
Michael, 11, 30, 37, 39, 53, 90, 93,
    94
Michah, 61
Michel, 42
Midian, 64
Mike, 94
Milo, 22, 90
Milton, 28, 29, 47, 86, 94
Misha, 54
Mishma, 64, 65
Mitchell, 30, 45, 53
Mizzah, 65
Moe, 37, 41, 53
Moise, 53
Moishe, 28, 42, 80
Monte, 104
Montgomery, 104
Mor, 74
Mordecai, 80, 104
Mordechai, 77
Moritz, 51
Morris, 22, 41, 104
Mortimer, 53
Morton, 28, 29, 47, 53
Moses, 22, 37, 41, 53, 61, 66, 104
Moshe, 61, 80
Motke, 80
Mottele, 80
Murray, 28, 47, 50, 53, 94
Murry, 51

Mushy, 104
Myron, 28, 47, 94

Nahath, 64
Nahum, 80
Naor, 71
Naphish, 65
Nat, 41, 94, 104
Nathan, 22, 50, 61, 94
Nathaniel, 22, 61, 67, 90, 104
Navon, 71
Ned, 22, 90
Nehemiah, 22
Neil, 94
Nethaniah, 64
Nicholas, 35, 67
Nick, 97
Nissan, 77
Nitzam, 74
Niv, 71
Noa, 70
Noah, 22, 37, 61, 66
Noam, 22, 37, 71
Noel, 90
Norman, 45, 53
Nufar, 74
Nun, 66
Nur, 71
Nuri, 71
Nusan, 42

Obadiah, 64
Offer, 71
Oliver, 22, 90
Omar, 61
Omer, 74, 77
Oran, 71
Oren, 22, 71, 74
Orin, 51, 71
Orli, 71
Orson, 22
Oscar, 53
Otto, 51
Owen, 90
Oz, 22

Parker, 11
Patrick, 28
Paul, 22, 53, 67, 90, 104
Peleg, 65
Pessel, 80
Peter, 22, 67, 90
Phil(l)ip, 39, 53, 67, 90, 104
Phineas, 22, 61
Pildash, 65
Pinchaul, 61
Pinnie, 80

Ralph, 53
Randy, 104
Rapha, 64
Raphael, 23, 61, 90
Raviv, 71
Raz, 71
Razi, 71
Raziel, 71
Red, 93, 98

Reed, 90
Reichan, 74
Rene, 104
Reuben, 23, 61, 104
Rex, 23, 90
Richard, 105
Rimon, 74, 76, 77
Rodney, 94
Roger, 45, 105
Ronald, 45, 105
Ronen, 71
Roni, 70
Roy, 45
Russell, 23, 90

Sagi, 71
Sam, 11, 29, 30, 33, 35, 36, 37, 90
Samson, 23, 61, 66
Samuel, 37, 90, 95, 97
Sander, 42, 51
Sandy, 98
Sanford, 105
Sasha, 54
Saul, 23, 37, 41, 61, 105
Schmuel, 28
Scott, 30, 45
Sean, 10
Selig, 8
Semon, 51
Seth, 23, 61, 90
Seymour, 3, 28, 32, 47
Shabat, 77
Shai, 71
Shaked, 73
Shamir, 71
Shaul, 61
Sheba, 66
Sheldon, 28, 29, 47
Shem, 64
Sherman, 47, 50
Shimon, 64
Shlomo, 42, 61, 105
Shmuel, 80
Shobab, 65
Shuppim, 66
Si, 41
Sid, 98
Sidney, 30, 47, 53, 95, 105
Siegmund, 51
Sigmund, 51, 105
Silas, 67
Sim, 41
Simchah, 79
Simeon, 23, 37, 61
Simm, 23, 37

Simon, 23, 37, 51, 67, 90
Sol, 41, 97
Solomon, 23, 51, 61
Soupy, 94
Spencer, 23, 90
Stanley, 3, 28, 29, 32, 47
Stav, 77
Stephen, 67, 90
Steve, 95, 105
Steven, 30, 45
Stewart, 45
Stuart, 45

Tabbai, 71
Tal, 71
Tamir, 71
Tammuz, 76, 77
Tebah, 64
Ted, 105
Tema, 64
Teman, 64
Terah, 64
Tevel, 81
Thaddeus, 67
Thahash, 65
Theodore, 52, 53
Thomas, 67
Tidhar, 73, 74
Timothy, 67
Tiras, 64
Titus, 67
Tobiah, 23
Tobias, 23, 61, 90
Tomer, 74
Tony, 93, 94
Treitel, 81
Tristan, 95
Tyler, 90
Tzabar, 74

Uri, 23, 71, 77
Uriah, 23, 61
Urijah, 64
Uz, 66
Uzi, 65

Victor, 45, 53, 94, 105

Walter, 45
Warren, 45
Will, 23, 90
William, 23, 39, 52, 53, 90, 105
Willie, 41
Winston, 10
Wolf, 52, 81

Woody, 93
Woolf, 105
Wyatt, 23

Yaad, 71
Yaal, 71
Yacov, 95
Yalon, 71
Yanek, 81
Yankel, 42, 81
Yaron, 71
Yasha, 81
Yezkhek, 81
Yisrael, 77
Yisroel, 42
Yitzhak, 61
Yitzroch, 95
Yoav, 64
Yona(h), 70, 76, 77
Yonatan, 71
Yonkel, 42, 55
Yonkele, 54
Yosef, 61
Yudel, 42
Yussel, 42

Zacchur, 64
Zachariah, 24
Zachary, 35, 90
Zaddok, 81
Zadok, 65
Zalman, 24, 42
Zamir, 71
Zayda, 8
Zayit, 74
Zebedee, 64
Zebediah, 24, 64
Zebulun, 65
Zedekiah, 24, 64
Zeftel, 79
Zellig, 81
Zephaniah, 64
Zer, 74
Zereth, 64
Zero, 95
Zev, 24
Zimram, 65
Zimri, 65
Ziph, 65
Zirel, 79
Zishe, 81
Ziv, 71
Zlateh, 79
Zohar, 71
Zvi, 24

ABOUT THE AUTHORS

LINDA ROSENKRANTZ is the author of the novel *Talk* and co-author of *Gone Hollywood* and *SoHo*. The former editor of *Auction* magazine, she now writes a nationally syndicated column on collectibles. She currently lives in Los Angeles with her husband and daughter.

PAMELA REDMOND SATRAN, former fashion features editor of *Glamour*, writes a syndicated column aimed at working parents. Her freelance articles have appeared in numerous publications, including *Self, Elle, Working Mother*, and *The Washington Post*. She lives with her husband, daughter, and son in London.

Their first collaborative work, *Beyond Jennifer & Jason*, was so popular that it spawned a series of specialized naming books, which also includes *Beyond Charles & Diana: An Anglophile's Guide to Baby Naming* and *Beyond Shannon & Sean: An Enlightened Guide to Irish Baby Naming*.